CRY JOY!

JERRY L. MERCER

VICTOR BOOKS®

A DIVISION OF SCRIPTURE PRESS PUBLICATIONS INC.
USA CANADA ENGLAND

Recommended Dewey Decimal Classification: 248.3
Suggested Subject Heading: SPIRITUAL LIFE

Library of Congress Catalog Card Number: 87-81013
ISBN: 0-89693-316-4

VICTOR BOOKS a division of SP Publications, Inc.
Wheaton, Illinois 60187

CONTENTS

To Ruth

Mystery Woman

Gift of God

Eternal Spring

FOREWORD

This Spiritual Formation book is for the Christian who hears God's call to a devotional life, and wants to better serve Him in the challenges of every day. It draws on the richness of Christian spirituality through the centuries of church history, but with an application to the twentieth-century believer who is involved in society, rather than withdrawn from it.

Spiritual Formation blends the best of traditional discipleship concepts with the more reflective disciplines of an individual journey toward friendship with God. It is a lifestyle, not a program; a relationship rather than a system; a journey instead of a roadmap. It calls us into holy partnership with God for our spiritual development.

As you read this book, and then others in the series, I hope that you will receive much more than information. My prayer is that you will experience new levels of formation of your mind and heart, and find yourself drawn closer to Christ.

Steven Harper, General Editor
Associate Professor of Spiritual Formation
Asbury Theological Seminary

PREFACE

Centuries ago, Nehemiah told the people of Israel that the joy of the Lord would be their strength. This is just as true today. Our happiness is in the Lord our God. His life in us is the joy that moves us from victory to victory in the spiritual life. Even when we face setbacks, as we will, it is the remembered joy of God's presence and blessing that pulls us back on our feet.

In the Beatitudes, the Lord Jesus described the life that pleases God in terms of happiness and hope. It is this life we are about to consider in *Cry Joy!* As you put these teachings into practice, you will discover yourself loving God in increasingly deeper ways. You will also find yourself relating better to other people and developing a naturally caring attitude toward them.

To live a happy or blessed life is to live with a supernatural joy which is not shaped by your outward circumstances. Actually, the joy of the Lord helps you shape your attitude toward your circumstances.

At the ends of the chapters, you will see meditations that will focus your attention on a main concern of what you have just read. It is not enough to read or even memorize the Beatitudes. They need to become food for your soul. They need to be your agenda for living, and this can happen only through meditation and prayer, as the Spirit who inspired the Beatitudes brings to light their special meaning for your life, and helps you willingly consent to God's ways.

Peace.

Jerry L. Mercer
Asbury Theological Seminary
Wilmore, Kentucky
1987

ONE

THE GREAT DISCOVERY

*J*esus, hope of the penitent
How kind You are to those who ask
How good You are to those who seek
What must You be to those who find?

—Bernard of Clairvaux[1]

Bernard's question, "What must You be to those who find?" is the driving force of authentic Christian faith. To know God in Christ is, as Augustine said, the chief end, or reason for living, of every person. There is within each of us a void which only God can fill. To know Christ is to complement the original acts of creation. We were all made to love and serve God. Jesus has come to make that relationship possible. Jesus has brought the life of God into the world so that those of us who have been redeemed may actually live the life of God. By grace we can be what God intended us to be by creation.

The life Jesus brings you and me is filled with happiness. The beautiful truth is that we can have it for the asking. It is God's gift to us, a gift God keeps on giving as long as we reach for it. This wonderful gift comes from the very heart of God. We all like to receive gifts on birthdays and special occasions. Some gifts are for the moment, like flowers or candy. Others, like clothes or appliances, may last a long time. But God's gifts are eternal. Asking of God, seeking God, finding God is a daily experience which lasts as long as we live, bringing us great happiness and satisfaction.

This magnificent joy of the Lord is a deep inner peace that makes all of life pleasing to God. It is a joy which causes our hearts to sing. It is a spiritual happiness given by the Holy Spirit to encourage us. It is the same kind of joy that strengthened our Lord as He approached the cross (Hebrews 12:2). This is indeed a "blessed" life—a life of victory over evil, of heartfelt love for God, and unbounded concern for everyone we meet.

I believe that the answer to Bernard's question can be found in the Beatitudes of Matthew's Gospel. If you really want to know what concerned Jesus most, you must read and reread these eight short summary statements that serve as an introduction to the Sermon on the Mount. The central theme of the Beatitudes is that *the life Jesus offers us is one of happiness and hope realized through our willing consent to God's ways.* These sayings show us how to grow in love for God and how to relate to others the same way God does. As we put these teachings into practice, we will discover ourselves loving God in increasingly deeper ways. We will also find ourselves relating better to other people and developing a naturally caring attitude toward them.

GOD'S GIFT TO SEEKING HEARTS

Early in His ministry our Lord withdrew one day to a mountain, probably to rest for a while. However, many people followed Him there because they were enamored with His teachings and His power to heal. The Lord decided to teach the people, and what He said we call the Sermon on the Mount. Jesus began,

> How blessed are the poor in spirit:
> the kingdom of heaven is theirs.

> Blessed are those who mourn:
> they shall be comforted.

> Blessed are the gentle:
> they shall have the earth as inheritance.

Blessed are those who hunger and thirst for
uprightness: they shall have their fill.

Blessed are the merciful:
they shall have mercy shown them.

Blessed are the pure in heart:
they shall see God.

Blessed are the peacemakers:
they shall be recognized as children of God.

Blessed are those who are persecuted in the
cause of uprightness: the kingdom of heaven is
theirs. [2]

It is very important that we pay attention to these special
teachings. The Beatitudes provide the milk of the Word for those
who are just beginning the spiritual way. They also provide the
meat of the Word for those who have been living with God for a
long time. You see, the Beatitudes meet us wherever we are in
Christ, guiding our spiritual growth in ways that please the Father.
We never outgrow our need of the Beatitudes. The more we live
them, the deeper they take us into the new reality which is Christ
in us, our hope of glory. The tremendous significance of the
Beatitudes is found in the life they produce—one of expanding
awareness of happiness and hope in Christ.

For all their apparent simplicity, the Beatitudes are not easy
for us to understand. Their meaning is somewhat hidden from us,
since we necessarily read them with a twentieth-century understanding. We do not think quite the same way as those who first
heard the Lord. As a result, we sometimes miss the thought patterns
so familiar to first-century Jews. They would have made connections between Jesus' teachings and their own history and spirituality, connections we naturally fail to make. Therefore, in order for
us to get maximum benefit from our Lord's teachings, we will look

at them in the light of their religious and social background. In this way the first century will inform the twentieth. One of the principal things we will learn in doing this is how similar our basic needs are to the needs of those who listened intently to our Lord that day on the mountainside.

GENUINE HAPPINESS

In my years of service for our Lord I have seen Him turn anger into compassion, stinginess into generosity, lust into caring, pride into humility, and despair into joy. In a word, Jesus takes unhappy, broken lives and remakes them into happy, healthy lives. This is truly the blessed life, the life of the Beatitudes, a life that has

> the Father as its Center,
> the Son as its Saviour,
> the Spirit as its Teacher,
> happiness as its basic mood,
> the kingdom of God as its final home!

No wonder Jesus calls such a life blessed. And to be so blessed is to be happy in the best sense of that word. In fact, the word *blessed* in the Beatitudes can be translated "happy" without losing any of its basic meaning.

> Happy are the poor in spirit . . .
> Happy the mourners . . . the gentle . . .
> Happy those who yearn for God . . .
> Happy are the merciful . . .
> the pure in heart . . . the peacemakers . . .
> those persecuted for living God's way.

Clarence Jordan caught the spirit of Gospel happiness in his translation of Paul's joy in Ephesians 1:3, "Three cheers for our Lord Jesus Christ's Father-God, who through Christ has cheered us along the heavenly way with every possible encouragement!"³

Yes, three cheers is right! All of us who have been changed by the Lord know that happiness and relief were among our first feelings on meeting Christ. It is, therefore, unfortunate that translators tend to shy away from using the word *happy* to describe the life of the Beatitudes. For many people happiness seems to be equated with good feelings and the trappings of success. So we draw smiley faces and sing catchy tunes about "Happiness is. . . ." But the happiness Jesus brings is no cotton-candy affair. His happiness is a deep well-being resulting from repentance, an inward realization of joy in God, a contentment amid difficulties, fulfillment based on faith and hope, a passion-driven intimacy with God.

To live a happy or blessed life is to live with a supernatural joy which is not shaped by our outward circumstances. Actually, the joy of the Lord helps us shape our attitudes *toward* our circumstances. Living a life hidden with Christ in God keeps us from being cocky when everything is going right. Likewise, it keeps us from caving in emotionally when the bottom drops out from under us. The happiness of the Beatitudes is a stabilizing factor, providing strength and insight. It keeps us from being victimized by life, both at its best and at its worst. The happy life is therefore lived from the conviction that God's goodness is being worked out in our lives, regardless of what happens to us.

When we read the "blessed" statements of the Lord, we should understand them to mean deeply happy, joyous, inwardly content, and truly fulfilled. These phrases all convey the same idea: *to participate in the life of God is the greatest reality we can know!* To live with God is *to live!* Although these ways of understanding happiness often cause us to feel very good, they take us far beyond feelings. Christian history is filled with stories of people who were happy in God even though they suffered terribly. I suppose the supreme test of the happy life of the Beatitudes (as we will see pointedly in the last Beatitude) is to experience joy in God when there is absolutely no rational reason for it.

PATIENCE, HUMILITY, AND FAITH

At the end of each chapter in this book is a suggested meditation for your use. The meditation attempts to focus your attention on a main concern of the chapter you have read. It is not enough just to read or even to memorize the Beatitudes. They need to become food for our souls, and that can happen only through meditation and prayer. The Beatitudes need to become our agenda for living. Yet only the Spirit who inspired them can bring to light their special meaning for us. It becomes necessary then for us to exercise patience, humility, and faith as we try to apply the Beatitudes to our lives.

† Patience. We need to be patient because there are no instant saints! A student in his late twenties said that he was dissatisfied with Christian faith because he had tried it and it had not brought about the changes in his life that he wanted. This was certainly a hasty conclusion. The recorded lives of some of the first Christians show us people who struggled with problems most of their lives. In the quest for a spiritual life, patience is a much-needed virtue.

Spiritual life, like physical growth, takes time. The Beatitudes do not give us an easy three-step method to spiritual gianthood. While it is certainly true that we will probably have moments of dramatic insight and change, our lives in God are bracketed with the humdrum routines of daily life. Many would-be Christians fall by the wayside because they expect too much too soon and quickly become disillusioned when growth doesn't occur according to their timetable. Thank God the student I mentioned above came to his senses and quit trying to rush what God was doing with him.

† Humility. We need to cultivate humility in spiritual growth because we are naturally defensive and tend to think we know more

about God than we actually do. We can be sure we have experienced great grace when we no longer feel the need to continually correct others in their experience of God. We need to resist the almost overpowering temptation to quickly assume that people who do not know God as we do are out in left field somewhere. Of course, we should be very careful to hold to the basic creeds of the Church. But it is healthy for us to be a bit suspicious of our own insights and motives. None of us are quite as gifted as we think we are or as pure in our motives as we want others to believe.

† Faith. Simple faith in God is crucial since most of us are inclined to want easy answers to our problems. Yet we know there are times when the events of our lives are shrouded in mystery; good reasons for what we are going through escape us. Sometimes our situation seems paradoxical in the light of our faith. At the seminary where I teach, we have found that young pastors often feel insecure unless they have a lot of ready-made answers for the hard places in the lives of their parishioners. But questions like, "Why do good people have to suffer?" or, "I have faith; why doesn't God heal me?" have no easy answers.

The spiritual life we need to develop goes beyond such questions, as pressing as they may seem. The basic point of spiritual awareness is to move from Why? questions to Yes! responses to God. We need to spend less time asking impossible questions and more time intensifying our relationship with the Father. Only by doing this can we become comfortable with mystery and learn to trust God's good providence to work out the tangles and discords of our lives.

Centuries ago, Nehemiah told the people that the joy of the Lord would be their strength (8:10). This is just as true today as it was in the days of restoration. Our happiness is in the Lord our God. His life in us is the joy that moves us from victory to victory. Even when we face setbacks, as we will, it is the remembered joy of God's presence and blessing that pulls us back on our feet. You and

CRY JOY!

I can rejoice that the Lord Jesus described the life that pleases God in terms of happiness and hope. It is that life we are about to study.

A MEDITATION OF PREPARATION

God, You are my God; I pine for You;
my heart thirsts for You,
my body longs for You
as a land parched, dreary and waterless.

Psalm 63:1

OBSERVE A TIME OF SILENCE

BEATITUDE

It happened that as [Jesus] was speaking, a woman in the crowd raised her voice and said, "Blessed the womb that bore You and the breasts that fed You!" But He replied, "More blessed still are those who hear the Word of God and keep it!"   Luke 11:27-28

A THOUGHT FOR MEDITATION

Teachers of the Lord's way agree that three things are necessary for beatitude: humility of heart, eagerness to learn, and readiness to obey.

To what extent are those characteristics of vital faith true in my life?

OBSERVE A TIME OF PRAYER

CLOSING READING

Matthew 12:46-50

T W O

SAYING YES TO HAPPINESS

*H*ow blessed are the poor in spirit:
the kingdom of heaven is theirs.

When my wife, Ruth, returned from a missions trip to the country of Belize, she brought home a deeply moving poem written by twelve-year-old Mawldyn Davies.

> Foodless children,
> With stomachs puffed out,
> Why do you have no food to eat?
> Why do you beg?
>
> Foodless children,
> Suffering from starvation,
> Why is your skin like paper?
> Why do your bones poke out?
>
> Foodless children,
> Eaten up by disease,
> Why not see a doctor?
> Why not?
>
> Foodless children,
> You are so thin,
> Your eyes are so appealing,
> And you will soon be dead.

The heart of the poem is a series of pathetic questions asked of the dying children: Why do you have no food to eat?

Why do you beg? Why is your skin like paper? Why do your bones poke out? Why not see a doctor?

How does a child, glassy-eyed and too weak to brush away the flies from his face, comprehend such questions, much less answer them? What then would his parents say—parents who themselves are hungry, dirty, and tired? What does a mother think, as helplessly she watches the life ebb slowly and painfully out of her child? The answers to Mawldyn Davies' questions cannot come from the dying, but from the living. From the perspective of the advantaged, answers are easy and obvious: the poor, especially in third-world countries, are victimized by a lack of technology, by natural disaster, or by ignorance.

The answers of the advantaged are neat and clean, and have a ring of truth in them. But the horrifying reality is beyond all that. The primary answer to poverty is in our hearts. It is an answer choked with our greed, our hunger for power, and our lust for control. It is an answer whose face is fear, party spirit, and war.

The poor are seen in the mirrors on our wall. When we ask who is the fairest of them all, if we look deeply, we will see the lean face of desperate human need staring back at us. We are shocked, for the lean face is our own. The poor, wherever they are found and however they got that way, are constant reminders of the fractured nature of our social order and the terrible selfishness of our own hearts. The skeletal bodies of the poor are likenesses of our own skeletal spirits. And this is the backdrop against which the first beatitude of Jesus must be understood.

RECOGNIZING OUR NEED OF REPENTANCE

The poor flocked to Jesus, hoping against hope He could change their miserable fortunes for the better. They knew they had great needs and there seemed to be no one else they could turn to for help. Jesus healed their diseases, raised their dead, and soothed their broken hearts. More than this He reminded them that God had not forgotten them, that even in their poverty they could be elevated to the status of children of God if only they would have faith. Many received His words as assurance from God that, at least in the long run, justice and mercy would prevail.

Like the Prophet Zephaniah (2:3), Jesus saw the needs of the people as a sign of a deeper, harsher reality. The poor represented the destitute condition of the human soul without God. Just as the physically poor turned to Jesus for deliverance, so must the spiritually poor. Indeed, there is nowhere else for the spiritually destitute to go. Gospel happiness begins with the painful admission that without God, one's life is all hopelessness and vanity. Those who become happy citizens of the kingdom of God are looking to Jesus to meet their overpowering sense of spiritual need.

Jesus gave a powerful example of this truth as He told of two men who went to the temple on the Sabbath for prayers (Luke 18:9-14). One was a respected member of the community, a Pharisee. He was known and admired for his learning in the sacred texts and for his obvious spirituality. The other man was despised by the people because he was a tax collector. It was generally assumed that tax collectors were social leeches, bleeding the people for their own gain.

"I thank You, God," the Pharisee prayed, "that I am not grasping, unjust, adulterous like everyone else, and particularly that I am not like this tax collector. I fast twice a week. I pay tithes on all I get."

To prove his point, the Pharisee rehearsed his good works, his fasting and tithing especially. Unlike the "grasping" tax collector, the Pharisee prided himself on his generosity. What the Pharisee said was probably true, but his self-righteousness canceled out any virtue he might claim. He was filled with pride, with the faulty assumption he was above everyone else, especially that man at the back of the room.

Whatever his sins against the community, and perhaps

because of them, the tax collector was a broken man. We are not told what guilts stirred his soul and brought him cowering to the temple. The story suggests he came to beg mercy from God. Unlike the Pharisee he exhibited his remorse by staying at the back of the temple area. He hung his head and looked at the floor. He beat his chest in utter anguish, blurting out one pitiful sentence: "God, be merciful to me a sinner."

As far as public opinion was concerned, both men were right. One was righteous and the other a sinner of the worst kind. Both should get what they deserved—reward for one and punishment for the other. And so it would be, Jesus said, but not according to common judgment. The Pharisee would go away smug but condemned, while the tax collector would go away repentant and forgiven! Jesus said that God approves of genuine humility which acknowledges sin and turns from it, but the door of the kingdom is locked tight against pride.

Happy are those who face the awful truth about themselves for God will take away their shame! That is the central lesson of this story. The poor in spirit are those who take a long look at their lives and are broken by what they see. This is not easy, as the tax collector shows us. It is agony to confess our need to God. We are like the Pharisee who looked around for someone to compare himself with, someone who would make him look good.

Our Lord said there are some people who turn and run from the light which He brings into the world. They much prefer to live in darkness. The basic reason is that they do not want to be exposed by His light. On the other hand, there are those who are so eager for truth that they want the light to shine on them. Lovers of darkness think that covering up their sins will make everything all right. They do not realize that to live in darkness is to live for death (John 3:19-21).

Jesus, the Light of the World, gives off so much brightness that the minutest details of our lives are shown up for what they are. The darkness is a temporary covering, but His light brings naked exposure. Those who come to the light prefer exposure, painful as it is. They know that hiding is a false comfort, and that it eventually destroys. Our only hope is exposure—coming to grips with what we are. This is not a one-time act of repentance after which we can say, "Thank God that is over." The closer to God we come, the more light there is and the more of ourselves we see. I am convinced the only thing that keeps us sane—as we really face ourselves—is the patient love of God which provides us security and a sense of acceptance.

The more we see ourselves, the more we realize that we are not as different from other people as we thought. We should never look down our noses in judgment on someone else, because we are fully capable of following them in their sins. We can sink into the various cover-ups, defenses and self-enhancing rationales, the same accusations of others, and constant casting of blame for our sins on others. But we cannot carry our covering, our darkness, into judgment. There, willing or not, we will be exposed and condemned. It is better to listen to the good word of Christ the Lord and enter now into the light of the saving Gospel.

Spiritual teachers in the church have long regarded pride as our basic problem. Pride shows up in almost every facet of our lives. My wife, Ruth, owns a bridal store. A consistent problem at the store is dress sizes; ladies often tell Ruth they are one size when in reality they may be much larger. Some customers are so touchy about this that they cannot accept the "tale of the tape," declaring up and down that the measurement is wrong. I am told by salespeople in men's stores that the same thing happens there.

If we have difficulty facing truth in such a small matter, should it surprise us that we find it almost impossible to face and admit our sins?

Some spiritual writers say pride stems from two kinds of ignorance—of human need and of God's ability to help. People filled with pride think they really do not need God in their lives.

They say, "I do not have needs that I cannot take care of myself."
The second group doubts that God is as necessary as He claims.
They say, "I prefer to be left alone with my own resources."

The way to the kingdom is to recognize one's need and
come to God for forgiveness and empowerment. The way to hear
words of pardon, comfort, and care from God the Father is to be
like the Publican and turn to God for mercy. To admit one's need
of God is part of the meaning of repentance. It is the first step
toward the kingdom.

POVERTY OF SPIRIT

There are some Christians who think their own pride is of the Holy
Spirit. We have all seen these people in the church. Many times I
have been approached by Christians who were absolutely sure they
had some special word or insight for me. Not one time has any of
these people asked about my own spiritual life. They simply
assumed it was inadequate, or lacking in the gifts of the Holy Spirit.
Thomas Merton's words of caution about this kind of spiritual
triumphalism are very important: "It is a terrible thing when such [a
person] gets the idea he is a prophet or a messenger of God or a
man with a mission to reform the world. . . . He is capable of
destroying religion and making the name of God odious to
[people]."

Sometimes these people are ministers of the church and
that compounds the problem, since they speak as recognized
authorities. Beware of any person who wants to make you his or her
disciple. Avoid those who are convinced that their spirituality is the
"right" one. Some forceful personalities think they are evangelists
for "God's way," when actually the way is their own.

Because Christians sometimes blow their experience of the
Lord out of proportion, and make all kinds of wild claims, we are
called by the Lord Himself to live a life of humility. A wise sage has
observed:

The greater you are,
the more humbly you should behave,
and then you will find favor with the Lord;
for great though the power of the Lord is,
He accepts the homage of the humble.[2]

To be poor in spirit is to live with the continual sense of
our total dependence on the mercy of God. So we will not be led
astray in this matter, the Apostle Paul urges us to make our own
"the mind of Christ Jesus," that is, to follow the pattern of life
modeled in Jesus. Paul says that the Lord,

being in the form of God,
did not count equality with God
something to be grasped.

But He emptied Himself,
taking the form of a slave,
becoming as human beings are;

And being in every way like a human being,
He was humbler yet,
even to accepting death, death on a cross.

For this God raised Him on high,
and gave Him the name
which is above all other names. . . .

Philippians 2:6-9

The Apostle Peter encourages us to put on humility as "the
garment you all wear constantly, because God opposes the proud
but accords His favor to the humble" (1 Peter 5:5). Paul says much
the same thing to the Colossians: "As the chosen of God, then, the
holy people whom He loves, you are to be clothed in heartfelt
compassion, in generosity and humility, gentleness and patience.
Bear with one another. . . . Put on love. . . . And may the peace of
Christ reign in your hearts" (3:12-15).

What flows through our minds when we think of the poverty of spirit lived out by Jesus? And also of the urging of Peter and Paul that we put on like a coat the same humble and obedient attitude of Jesus? It is true that Jesus was very hard on the interpreters of the law when they misconstrued the meaning of the tradition. But it is also true that He urged His followers to love one another, to be patient with everyone, to bear up under persecution, and to always conduct themselves as self-denying servants. Too often Jesus' selflessness seems impossible to understand, especially when we are self-protective, defensive, and eager to have our own way. The call to humble obedience issued by Paul is a lifelong process of bringing our desires and goals into line with Jesus' humility.

What does such a lifestyle of Gospel humility, of poverty of spirit, mean to us? If we listen carefully we might hear Jesus say something like:

> How deeply happy are those who are not occupied with themselves, but who constantly turn their attention to others.

> How deeply happy are those who do not boast of their accomplishments, but sincerely praise what others do.

> How deeply happy are those who love to serve people, who deny themselves to make others happy.

> How deeply happy are those who silently offer back to God the compliments they receive.

> How deeply happy are those who lean on God continually; God will comfort them now and forever.

INHERITING THE KINGDOM

Just as there are two levels of meaning to being poor in spirit, so there are two aspects to inheriting the kingdom. First, to inherit the kingdom means to live right now as one accepted by God through Jesus Christ. It means having the kingdom within our hearts as a living reality. The poor in spirit look to God for help and, much to their surprise, God gives them the kingdom! This means we are forgiven and become children of God. This is happiness indeed!

But the kingdom is also God's future for us. Christ is our loving King, and the new reality He has brought into the world is the first phase of the kingdom reign of God. God puts into our hearts a longing for the full manifestation of this inner kingdom, a longing which will be fulfilled sometime in the future. Thus, the kingdom of God in its fullness is the destiny of the church. This is certainly a reason for rejoicing. The future is not dark and hopeless, but is filled with promise.

This twofold aspect of the kingdom means we live between the times, so to speak. The kingdom is here in its infancy; it is coming in its maturity. Such hope helps us endure hardship and pain. This kingdom hope builds confidence that God will reconcile all the contradictions in our lives in His own time. This hope encourages us to look for the appearing of our Lord. In the world we experience frustration and disappointment because of evil. However, we do not despair, being confident of the kingdom to come. Some have seen these two phases of the kingdom as the "kingdom of grace" in the present and the "kingdom of glory" in the future. For now we are called to live in the kingdom of grace as fully as possible, waiting patiently for the kingdom of glory.

A PRAYER OF LETTING GO

Jesus told His disciples, "If anyone wants to be a follower of Mine, let him renounce himself and take up his cross and follow Me. Anyone who wants to save his life will lose it; but anyone who loses his life for My sake will find it (Matthew 16:24-25).

The heart of the spiritual life is to learn to think as the Lord thinks. This is what begins to happen when we accept the Lord into our hearts and learn to live the life He taught us. This learning process is a constant choosing of God's revealed way. We will always be faced with the responsibility of choosing the will of God. Likewise, we will be continually turning away from the influences of evil and turning toward God. This first Beatitude encourages us to choose God, to say yes to happiness.

I want to close this chapter with the Prayer of Abandonment written by the late Charles Foucauld. Foucauld was a missionary to the Touareg people of North Africa shortly after the turn of this century. His prayer is special to me because it shows the spirit of a man who labored faithfully for sixteen years without seeing even one convert. He was eventually killed by some of the Touareg during a time of hostility. Yet his self-denial did not go unrewarded. During those long years, Foucauld was busy reducing the language of the people to writing, producing dictionaries, and translating portions of Scripture. Today there is a thriving work among the descendants of the people to whom Foucauld preached in the name of Christ. The following prayer shows us how this man of God was able to stick with his commitment, even though it appeared that he was not accomplishing anything.

> Father,
> I abandon myself unto Your hands;
> do with me what You will.
> Whatever You may do, I thank You;
> I am ready for all, I accept all.
> Only let Your will be done in me,
> and in all Your creatures.
> I wish no more than this, O Lord.
> Into Your hands I commend my soul;
> I offer it to You with all the love of my heart,
> for I love You, Lord, and so need to give Myself,
> to surrender myself into Your hands, without reserve,
> and with boundless confidence,
> for You are my Father. [3]

A MEDITATION ON HUMILITY

Poor and needy as I am,
the Lord has me in mind.
You, my Helper, my Saviour
my God, do not delay.

Psalm 40:17

OBSERVE A TIME OF SILENCE

BEATITUDE

How blessed are the poor in spirit:
the kingdom of heaven is theirs.

A THOUGHT FOR MEDITATION

"We must be content to live without watching ourselves live, to work without expecting an immediate reward, to love without an instantaneous satisfaction, and to exist without any special recognition."

Thomas Merton[4]

True humility is the foundation upon which our spiritual life is built. A sense of spiritual poverty is the beginning of our life of prayer and service.

OBSERVE A TIME OF PRAYER

CLOSING READING

Matthew 11:28-30

THREE

KEEPING A WATCHFUL EYE

*B*lessed are those who mourn:
they shall be comforted.

When Jesus saw the crowds on the mountainside that day, His heart was moved with compassion. They had come to hear Him from every part of Palestine, even as far away as "the other side of Jordan." Jesus saw them as shepherdless sheep, wandering and lost. Some were probably just curious about this young carpenter's son; most were hopeful He could do something for them.

As Jesus' fame spread throughout Syria, "those who were suffering from disease and painful complaints of one kind or another, the possessed, epileptics, the paralyzed, were all brought to Him, and He cured them. Large crowds followed Him. . . . Everyone in the crowd was trying to touch Him because power came out of Him that cured them all" (Matthew 4:24-25; Luke 6:19).

The suffering came to Jesus, as they would until He was lifted above the earth outside the city walls of Jerusalem, drenched in His own peculiar agony. The crowd was made up of lepers, blind people, the deaf, those crazed by real or imagined spirits, epileptics, the twisted and bent, those for whom every movement was an act of pain and anguish. They had heard wild rumors of Jesus' power to heal. " 'Here is a teaching that is new, and with authority behind it: He gives orders even to unclean spirits and they obey Him.' And His reputation at once spread everywhere, through all the surrounding Galilean countryside" (Mark 1:27-28).

THOSE WHO MOURN

How would we describe the mourners Jesus saw? I think He saw people racked by the torments of psychotic episodes and actual possession by evil. Others were deeply guilt-ridden, consumed by repressed anger, sorrow, and shame. Some were maladjusted, social misfits, unable to function according to social expectations. Others were discouraged, perhaps depressed, sick inside because of generations of oppression by foreign powers, and deathly afraid of reprisals by the Romans. Of course, many of the mourners were physically distressed and emotionally drained.

Don't you find it interesting that the Gospel writers do not mention that the well-off, well-fed, satisfied-with-life who were there? I feel sure that some healthy, happy people were there, perhaps helping distraught friends who couldn't make it on their own. But for the most part, this crowd to whom our Lord spoke was discouraged, disadvantaged, and distressed. This whole episode is a graphic reminder that the Saviour came to deliver the helpless, and that the kingdom of God is made up of those redeemed from great problems. Under the best of circumstances, the early church was made up largely of those who were uneducated, who lacked political power—common people (1 Corinthians 1:26). In fact, God chose such people to inherit the kingdom to shame the supposed wisdom of the philosophers, politicians, and scientists. Citizens of the kingdom, then and now, are miracles of grace!

Those people who heard the Lord were not very different from us. You could gather the same kind of crowd in New York City or Los Angeles. Human need hasn't changed a good deal since the first century. Thirty minutes in any large hospital will show us more kinds of physical distress than were represented in the crowd that followed Jesus. We are just as fearful of invasion by our enemies as they were. Our lives, like theirs, are filled with deadening routine. At some time or other all of us think life meaningless and problematic. Newspaper accounts tell us of suicides from the slums and high society, and for the same reason! If anything, our problems are more exaggerated today because most of us are packed into urban centers.

The mourners of the first century were desperate and came to Jesus because they had exhausted other avenues of help. He was their last resort—and He is ours. It is when we reach a point of desperate need that we go to Jesus for help.

Jesus said that mourners were happy people! If that didn't cause His listeners to sit up and take notice, nothing would. They were very unhappy! How could they possibly be happy?

SORROW OVER SIN

The key that unlocks the meaning of this Beatitude is found in the words of the first Beatitude: *in spirit.* Jesus associated the word *mourn* with sorrow over sin—one's own sin and the sins of others. This would not have been lost on some in that crowd. The Old Testament contains many examples of mourning as sorrow over sin. In fact, there are more than forty Psalms of Lament, that is, psalms concerned with anxiety caused by breaking the covenant, the threat of enemies, and the fear of death.

Psalm 51 is a psalm of lament which focuses on the remorse of a sinning believer. It was written by a man who was so devastated before the Lord that his guilt followed him everywhere. His only recourse was confession; yet he was so ashamed that in his confession he asked God not even to look at him.

Have you ever felt like this? I know I have. Let's take a look at David's candid and emotional plea for forgiveness.

> Have mercy on me, O God, in Your faithful love,
> in Your great tenderness wipe away my offenses;
> wash me thoroughly from my guilt,
> purify me from my sin.
> For I am well aware of my offenses,

my sin is constantly in mind.
Against You, You alone, have I sinned,
I have done what You see to be wrong. . . .

But You delight in sincerity of heart. . . .
Purify me with hyssop till I am clean,
wash me till I am whiter than snow. . . .

Turn away Your face from my sins,
and wipe away all my guilt.

God, create in me a clean heart,
renew within me a resolute spirit. . . .

Give me back the joy of Your salvation. . . .

Sacrifice to God is a broken spirit,
a broken, contrite heart You never scorn.

God has given us a powerful conscience which serves as a
kind of barometer, indicating to us whether our attitudes and
actions are good or bad.

In one sense, conscience is the prompting of the Spirit of
God. Unless we have deadened our conscience through repeated
and willful acts of sin, feelings of guilt are often God's way of
getting us back on the right track.

The psalmist says that God never scorns a "broken, contrite
heart." Why? When real guilt is too much to handle, our defenses
come down and we begin to be honest about ourselves. Our feeling
is that we should be punished for what we have done. But there
comes a point where punishment is better than the pain of trying to
hide our sins. God is not put off by our confession; He is not
embarrassed by our admission of guilt, even if we have done
something terrible. God is a good Father who loves us. We should
not hesitate to bring our problems to Him.

The psalmist's idea of a broken heart has been understood
by some spiritual writers to mean that God wants His children to
maintain an attitude of brokenness before Him. This means that we

should always be ready to confess our sins, however small they may seem, and should always be alarmed at the thought of disobeying the will of God. Jesus' Beatitude on mourning teaches us that a life of personal examination and watchfulness against sin produces a sense of freedom and happiness in God. Without this assurance from the Lord, Christian spirituality would seem morbid and depressing. However, those who have faithfully practiced self-examination know the joy it brings.

An example of what I mean can be found in Francis of Assisi's prayer before the crucifix in the church of San Damiano. Shortly after he had given up everything to follow the Lord, he was praying in this broken-down church, seeking the Lord's guidance. During this time he heard the voice of God speaking to him from the painted crucifix, telling him to repair the church—meaning to revive the Roman Catholic Church's zeal for true spiritual life.

Francis' response to the voice was a prayer which characterized his life. It is a plea that God would dispel darkness (ignorance and sin) and fill his heart with faith, hope, and love.

Most high,
glorious God,
enlighten the darkness of my heart,
and give me, Lord,
a correct faith,
a certain hope,
a perfect charity,
sense and knowledge,
so I may carry out Your holy and true command. [1]

How does God "enlighten the darkness" of our hearts and give us the grace we need to please God? According to Francis, by giving us Holy Wisdom, Pure Holy Simplicity, Holy Poverty, Holy Humility, Holy Charity, and Holy Obedience. [2]

CRY JOY!

Francis capitalized the gifts from God because he regarded these virtues as divine friends, not mere attitudes. He prefaced them with the word *holy*, and when their holiness is kept in mind:

> Wisdom becomes our knowledge of God, a knowledge based on faith.
>
> Simplicity becomes a life lived for God's glory alone, not for self-glory.
>
> Poverty becomes self-denial in order to give to meet the needs of others.
>
> Humility becomes an attitude of constant reverence toward God.
>
> Charity becomes the desire to serve God by serving others.
>
> Obedience becomes our heart's desire to please God in everything we think, say, and do.

Not only are these virtues means through which our darkened hearts are enlightened by God, but they also act as guardians of our souls—keeping them holy before God.

> Holy Wisdom destroys the tricks of the devil,
> Pure holy Simplicity destroys worldly wisdom,
> Holy Poverty destroys our love of the world,
> Holy Humility destroys pride,
> Holy Charity destroys temptation and fear,
> Holy Obedience destroys self-will.

Francis believed that a prayer for light becomes effective as we humble ourselves before God in a spirit of brokenness and confession. Enlightenment and guardianship produce great happiness, perhaps even occasional overflowing love. To pray to God in this spirit is to take careful stock of oneself. It is also to become a watchful person, being very careful not to intentionally sin against the will of God. It is to keep our spiritual eyes open against the wiles of sin and uplifted toward God.

SELF-EXAMINATION

We maintain a spirit of watchfulness and prayer through the discipline of self-examination. This idea should not be strange to us, since we are always evaluating our performance in one way or another. As a teacher I am continually evaluated as to my readiness for class, depth of preparation, and classroom performance. Salespeople, factory workers, corporation executives are all evaluated as to their performance on the job. Spiritual self-examination is taking stock of our lives in the light of the biblical revelation. This exercise is most helpful when done with a spiritual friend or guide, but can be done with profit alone, as well.

The idea of self-examination is to find those places in our lives where we need help. We do not examine ourselves in order to pat ourselves on the back for doing good. It is important to always remember that we are sinners being redeemed by the sheer grace of God. Jonathan Edwards, the great Puritan scholar and pastor, practiced a rugged type of self-examination, checking himself every evening against a list of sixty-seven attitudes and actions which he believed pleased God. Most of the items came from the New Testament—concerns such as not being judgmental, being honest, and seeking holiness of heart. He would go over this list in prayer to see if he had missed the mark anywhere. With a list as long as he had, he was bound to find some problem area in his life for that day. For Edwards, confession was very important since it opened him up to the cleansing grace of God.

On first glance we might regard Jonathan Edwards' discipline as depressing. But he knew the human tendency to justify bad attitudes and behaviors. He also knew that the devil is our enemy and that evil actively tries to keep us from God.

The reason for self-examination, regardless of the length of our list, is that we might be made aware on a deep level of who we really are before God. In this way we are forcefully reminded that all our hopes for happiness depend entirely on the Lord. If we become discouraged about what we uncover in our lives, then we should recall that Christ died and rose again in order that we might be redeemed.

In a period of self-examination, we can use as a guide any portion of Scripture that teaches what it means to love and serve God, such as a psalm, the words of Jesus, the teachings of Paul, John, and other writers. The idea is to ask questions of the text and then to ask questions about ourselves. Jesus prayed,

> Our Father in heaven,
> may Your name be held holy,
> Your kingdom come,
> Your will be done,
> on earth as in heaven.
> Give us today our daily bread.
> And forgive us our debts,
> As we have forgiven those
> who are in debt to us.
> And do not put us to the test,
> but save us from the Evil One.
>
> Matthew 6:9-13

We will ask only a few questions of this prayer, enough to show how it might be used. Let us ask if we have held the name of God holy in our thoughts and words throughout the day. By holy, Jesus meant for us to keep the name of God lifted up in our thoughts and unstained by what we say. The Jews believed the divine name contained the essence of God, and was far more than a description of God. The name Yahweh suggests something of the may mean, "I am who I am," or "I will be what I will be," or "I am becoming what I will become." This name is so majestic that mysterious nature of God. Its literal translation is very difficult. It Orthodox Jews will not say it, using "Lord" instead. To speak lightly of God's name means more than using it in cursing or jokes. It means doubting God's faithfulness or disregarding His covenant. The divine name is so elevated that Paul said we will all bow before it on the day of judgment.

But let's go on with our self-examination, to our treatment of others. In the model prayer we ask for forgiveness from God *to the same extent* that we forgive people who have wronged us. This is so important to Jesus that He repeats it after the prayer is finished (Matthew 6:14-15).

Now let us examine our consciences on this point. Have we forgiven the failings of others? Or have we held back because the issue was "too personal" or "too serious"? If we can say honestly that we have forgiven our friends and relatives, what about our enemies? Have we forgiven them of what they have done or tried to do to us? Do we pray for them, do good to them, love them? Remember, if we do not forgive freely, God will not forgive us. Furthermore, if we set aside this teaching, or any part of it, we have become guilty of not keeping God's name holy—we think we can ignore His direct teaching if we choose to.

We have only begun to reflect on the Lord's Prayer as a means of self-examination and already we sense our guilt. Honest self-examination reveals flaws in us and provides for confession and growth. Such self-examination results in great blessing, because we are allowed by the Father to penetrate both ourselves and the reality of God. This in turn produces unbounded happiness. I am sure that self-examination, properly mourning over sin in our lives and the lives of others, is a vital part of growing spiritually. Such self-examination and repentance help us avoid false triumphalism. And we can take heart that it is the sick who are made well, the beggars who are fed.

A LIVING JOY

Those who are genuinely alarmed at sin in themselves and in others are joyous, because God will deliver them from sin. Jesus' promise is that the mourners will be comforted! This certainly happens whenever we bring our sins to Christ. We have the assurance that He forgives them. We are confident because the Bible says sins genuinely confessed are forgiven. Also there is the witness of the Holy Spirit to our hearts that grace and life are at work in us, and not condemnation and death.

Of course, there is the joy ahead, the crown of righteousness, the future rest, the place where all tears are wiped away. The kingdom of glory or heaven is the final goal of all authentic faith. And the reason heaven will be heaven is not because our friends or relatives will be there, but because it is there we will be allowed to experience the reality of God in an unhindered way. Heaven will be our greatest comfort because of the marriage supper of the Lamb, when the church (you and I, and all the redeemed) will be presented to Christ as His spotless bride. And He will love us for all eternity, as at a great wedding feast of love.

Jesus makes it clear that the life of mourning over sin is a happy life. This happiness comes because of our sincere desire to avoid evil. This "calm, inward joy," as one spiritual writer puts it, in no way depends on the varying circumstances of life. Having the Father as its foundation, the Son as its redeemer, and the Spirit as its energizer, this happiness is also different from anything produced in our life in the world.

Such mourners see into the reality of things and are jarred by their vision, for it strips them of all claims to self-righteousness. Now there is only turning, constant and intense; purging of earthbound values; denial of the applause of the crowd, rejection of the temptation to have it one's own way. To mourn is to look through one's personal void to God, and to see beyond despair a living joy which blesses life with happiness and hope.

A MEDITATION ON CONFESSION

Down in the dust I lie prostrate;
true to Your word, revive me.
I tell You my ways and You answer me;
teach me Your wishes.
Show me the way of Your precepts,
that I may reflect on Your wonders.
I am melting away for grief;
true to Your word, raise me up.

Psalm 119:25-28

OBSERVE A TIME OF SILENCE

BEATITUDE

Blessed are those who mourn:
they shall be comforted.

A THOUGHT FOR MEDITATION

"Only God is, only God knows, only God can do anything. This is the
truth, and with the help of my faith I discover this more deeply every
day."   Carlo Carretto[3]

We are not wise enough, good enough,
or strong enough to gain favor with God.
Forgiveness comes as a sheer gift.

OBSERVE A TIME OF PRAYER

CLOSING READING

Romans 13:8-10

FOUR

LISTENING TO GOD

*B*lessed are the gentle:
they shall have the earth as
inheritance.

All of us bring distorted attitudes and expectations into our experience of God. Several years ago I had a student who was an ex-military man, all spit and polish. He was exact in his mannerisms, sometimes abrupt, and could take control of the class almost at will. He did respect authority and therefore deferred to me, but other students felt intimidated by him. One class session obviously touched a raw nerve in this young man—the day we discussed the idea of meekness or gentleness.

"I'm not going to be a wimp for Christ!" he said adamantly.

I suggested to him that he could not shape the blessed life to suit himself, which in his case would be a strong, no-nonsense approach. His military bias interpreted meekness as weakness and he wanted no part of that. He wanted to be God's warrior instead. He wanted to be a *man*. Try as I might, I could not help him see that by *gentle*, Jesus did not mean wimpish. Finally I cautioned him against saying what he would or would not be in God's service, for I was sure God would put him to the test precisely at that point, to bring him to submission and humility.

For my young friend the masculine ideal was tied up with toughness and the ability to conquer, characteristics the first-century Jews wanted to see in the Messiah. The student's reaction, all too common among males, is a perfectly natural reaction, because the influence of our past tells us to be wary of others. In an attempt to cope with our fears of other people, we tend to become defensive and self-protective. Such distortions make it very difficult for us to relate easily to the teachings of Jesus. In fact, were it not for the grace of God, this would be absolutely impossible!

THE GENTLE SPIRIT

The meaning of this Beatitude is difficult to grasp because several ideas are wrapped up in the word *gentle*. Depending on the scriptural context within which the word is used it might mean one of the following:

> The gentle do not demand having their own way all of the time.
>
> The gentle want to be unassuming in the presence of others.
>
> The gentle are eager to conform to God's expectations.
>
> The gentle always want to live graciously with others.
>
> The gentle have a calm trust in the providence of God.

In this Beatitude, Jesus is trying to show us that Gospel happiness comes to those who listen attentively to God. The gentle are those who want their perspectives on life to be shaped by God's will alone. You might say the gentle hold fast to whatever God wants, however much it might contradict what they have been taught. The gentle are those who do not want to have a private will apart from God's will. Whatever pleases the Father pleases them. To live this way means to intentionally give ourselves to be shaped by God's love.

Of course, such teaching seems foreign in a culture that emphasizes a take-charge approach to getting ahead in life. But Jesus sees that we will not be able to handle power until we come to grips with who we really are before God. Like the two previous Beatitudes, this teaching is concerned first of all with our attitude toward God. Only those who are poor in spirit, and are alarmed over their sins, can even begin to approach the depth of this Beatitude.

Our Lord may have had Psalm 37:11 in mind as He gave this teaching on gentleness: "But the meek shall inherit the earth; and shall delight themselves in the abundance of peace" (NKJV).

The Hebrew word for *meek* in this psalm probably means "poor" or "humiliated." Understood this way, the psalm would encourage Jews who were in the throes of depression because their nation had been overrun by enemies. "Things look glum for the present," the psalmist says, "but take heart. God has not forgotten His people. The meek or humiliated ones must have confidence in God. Trust God! Do what He says! God will save those who take refuge in Him."

What a wonderful teaching and how necessary, not only for the ancient Jews but for us as well. If you and I are truly searching for gentleness of heart and are listening attentively to what God says, then we can have confidence that God will work things out. Such trust will enable us to rejoice in the midst of difficulties. We will learn to be patient and wait for the day of deliverance God has ahead of us. Because we want God's will in everything, we will never give up hope.

Undoubtedly some who heard this Beatitude thought of the Ten Commandments, for it reflects the words of Deuteronomy 4:1-2, as the Old Testament writer urges the people to accept the Commandments at face value, not altering them in any detail: "You must add nothing to what I command you, and take nothing from it, but keep the commandments of Yahweh your God just as

I lay them down for you."

The people were to lay aside their own will on these Commandments and carefully follow the instructions of the Lord. Failure to do this would result in the loss of their land. Faithful obedience of the Commandments would keep the nation secure. The lesson here is that happiness and security are found in doing the will of God, the Creator of heaven and earth.

The heart of this third Beatitude can be seen in the stone wall of the guesthouse of a Roman Catholic monastery not far from my home. Etched in the facing are the words, "God Alone." These words tell everyone who comes to the monastery for a retreat, whether laborer, executive, or college student, that they are to seek only God as the center of their lives and the source of their help. The same idea is reflected in the slogan for the youth fellowship of a large Protestant denomination, "Christ Above All." The gentle ones of Jesus' Beatitude are people who genuinely seek to listen to God and do what pleases Him.

I will never forget the testimony I heard from a young woman at a prayer session. Her marriage was teaching her the meaning of this Beatitude.

> Before I was married, I continually thought of God's love and grace. No matter what I was doing I seemed able to reflect on God. Then I met the man who is now my husband and we fell in love. But my attention was now divided between God and my husband. In some ways my devotional life began to slack off and my joy in the Lord diminished. Then it dawned on me that even though I was happily married, I would have to be as a single person in my devotion to my Lord. Now my husband has become a part of my life of praise to the Lord and God is once more the center of my life.

This Christian woman learned all over again what it means

to seek God only. Listening to God enhanced her marriage and brought her greater happiness. She was learning to live in Jesus' new standard of goodness.

THE NEW STANDARD OF GOODNESS

Listening to God means living with a new standard of goodness. This is considerably more than being merely a law-abiding citizen or even a responsible church member. A person may obey the law of the land but not be particularly happy about it or attend worship services and go through the motions without heart involvement. But true goodness encompasses both attitude and action. The goodness Jesus teaches comes from a seeking heart.

Jesus gave an example of this when He said our goodness should go beyond that of the Pharisees (Matthew 5:20). The Pharisees were very strict on keeping the letter of the Law, whether or not their heart was in it. This did not satisfy God, Jesus said. God wants us to obey Him because we genuinely want to.

This new standard of goodness spoken of by the Lord is what Dietrich Bonhoeffer called "simple, unreflecting obedience to the will of Christ."[1] Such obedience is "simple" because it focuses all its attention on what Christ teaches us to do. Such simplicity means that God is the primary content of our lives and that God's will is the single desire of our hearts.

This obedience is also self-denying in that we act on what God says without reflection. If God says it, we do it—we are His people and we know His will is best. To do what God says without debating about it is a high standard. Such obedience comes from a heart absolutely convinced that it is to our advantage to do what God's will teaches us.

The single-minded desire to listen to God produces a heart motivated by God's love. Jesus illustrated this in an example on telling the truth (Matthew 5:33-37). It is assumed in our courts, as it was also in the first century, that persons are more likely to give honest testimony if they swear by something. So we place our hand on the Bible and take an oath that we will not lie. Jesus says it is unnecessary for His followers to take such an oath because their simple yes or no will be the truth. Those who listen only to God do not have to be pressured into telling the truth. They tell the truth because they want to do the will of the God of truth.

Jesus' second example of goodness seems especially mean-ingful to Christians today who live in a world threatened by terrorism and war. We are to love our enemies and pray for those who persecute us. Caring acts of love are to be given to our enemies so that we may be children of our Father in heaven. The Lord continued, "You must therefore set no bounds to your love, just as your Heavenly Father sets none to His" (Matthew 5:48).

The gentle say, "If this is what God wants, by His grace we will do it!" Certainly this is not a position of weakness. It is rather one of strength and courage in wanting to follow God's will, even though it seems to contradict social convention and common sense.

But what will love and kindly prayers do in such a situa-tion? That is for God to decide. Dietrich Bonhoeffer, himself a target of Nazi cruelty during World War II, helps us with our perspective.

> No sacrifice which a lover would make for his beloved is too great for us to make for our enemy. If out of love for our brothers we are willing to sacrifice goods, honor and life, we must be prepared to do the same for our enemy. We are not to imagine that this is done to condone his evil; such a love proceeds from strength rather than weakness, from truth rather than fear; and therefore, it cannot be guilty of hatred of another.[2]

The love Jesus demands is radical love! The goodness He expects is a demanding goodness! Only the gentle, those deter-mined to do only God's will, are given the ability to do what Jesus' new standard of goodness requires. To love like this calls for personal resolve and the power of the Holy Spirit.

This kind of gentleness was reflected in the lives of the early followers of Francis of Assisi. Franciscan history is filled with stories of Francis' desire to love God with all his heart, and to show kindness to everyone he met, friend and foe alike. The spirit of Francis, and of this Beatitude, is seen in the following exhortation to goodness by Brother Giles, one of Francis' close companions.

> If you love, you will be loved.
> If you fear, you will be feared.
> If you serve, you will be served.
> If you treat others well, others will treat you well.

> Blessed is he who loves
> and does not therefore desire to be loved.
> Blessed is he who fears
> and does not therefore need to be feared.
> Blessed is he who serves
> and does not therefore desire to be served.
> Blessed is he who treats others well
> and does not therefore desire
> that others treat him well. [3]

INHERITING THE EARTH

Jesus says those who listen to God will inherit the earth. Palestine was considered "the land of promise" by first-century Jews, the land promised by God to Abraham their ancestor. As such the land was a gift to the Jews since, according to their belief, everything belonged to God and it was God's to give. To receive the land as a gift was in essence to receive as a gift what belongs to God.

I am sure Jesus did not mean that those who love God can lay claim to a particular property. This is not the point. Inheriting the earth must be understood as first of all a spiritual truth about the kingdom within.

John Wesley thought to inherit the earth in this spiritual sense meant to live a contented life without much regard for the shifting circumstances around us; to be satisfied with what we have and not be eager to always have more and more.[4] Is your house adequate for your family needs? If so, do not enlarge it. Are plain clothes warm and comfortable? Then do not buy outlandish and expensive clothes. Do you have more money than you need to secure the well-being of your family and business? Then give the excess to those who need it more than you do. For Wesley, contentment was the opposite of greed. To be happy with what was adequate was to inherit the earth. Only those whose desire was to please God were not to some degree grasping and greedy.

I believe Wesley was basically right. Our primary needs are few. By trimming our desires to match our real needs, we can live comfortably with less. Possessions often bring worry with them. This tends to make goods more important than they really are. To keep goods, and life in general, in their proper place is to experience a freedom that some spiritual writers call "living without care." To live without care means to live free of the consuming desire to always have more. Living this way makes it possible for us to help those who have little or nothing. In this sense, to inherit the earth is to honor the love God has for all the people of the earth.

We also inherit the earth when our eyes and hearts are opened to what Charles Cummings calls "the mystery of the ordinary."[5] Much of the time we are too preoccupied to "stop and smell the roses." Cummings believes our spiritual lives will be enriched if we give attention to such ordinary activities as walking, eating, resting, even hurting. To give attention to these things is to meditate on their importance to human life. It is to recognize the wisdom and goodness of God in providing for the expansion of our experience of the natural world, as well as the world of our everyday activities.

Francis of Assisi was keenly aware that nature and human life are gifts of God's love. He gave away all his earthly goods in order that he might possess all the earth. For him owning nothing meant owning everything. He often danced on the hills and sang praise to the God who gives a simple and wonderful life. He called the animals his brothers and sisters, as he did the sun, moon, and stars. At his request he died naked on the earth. Even in death Francis demonstrated his belief that the natural world is basically good and a gift of God.

When was the last time you sat and watched a beautiful sunrise or sunset? Did it lift your thoughts to God? Have you thought to thank God for sleep and its renewing power? Do you know the delicious feeling of seeing something you really wanted and could afford, and turning and walking away from it, thanking God for giving you the ability to turn loose of a strong desire? To inherit the earth is to live freely with earth's rhythms. It is to take delight in the earth, seeing it as a dim reflection of the majesty and power of our Father in the heavens.

There is a tinge of the future in Jesus' words as well. The inheritance of the earth is a hope for oppressed peoples. The promise of the new heavens and earth in Revelation 21–22 corresponds to this future for God's people. The earth is God's to give and ours to enjoy. When the human enjoyment of the earth's bounty is cut short by greed and war, then we must take refuge in God's promise that the earth is not a prize to be won but a gift to be received. And those who receive it are those who seek to listen attentively to God's will and do it. Faithful obedience will receive the promise. This is a hope that fortifies us to stand for life and against those who restrict life.

THE ENEMY OF THE GENTLE

The gentle of the Lord must learn patience if they want to receive as a gift what belongs to God. As far as I can tell, Jesus never considered physical enemies to be a major threat to true spirituality. As the gentle, we can put up with our enemies. They are, after all, objects of our love. What we must be on guard against are spiritual enemies. And while there are many such enemies that plague us, "There is no greater obstacle to the presence of the Spirit in us than anger."[6]

Anger usually comes from a wounded ego. One objective of true spirituality is to be so changed by God that we react to life from the standpoint of love, not anger. This does not mean that anger is never warranted. Feelings of anger at a child molester are natural. Becoming angry at injustice and oppression can be a Christian response, if the anger is channeled into constructive action. Anger represents a tremendous inner force which can be turned to good use if we vent our anger by doing something that is just, that helps insure personal and social freedoms. The danger with anger is in our tendency to lash out unthinkingly, to react with uncontrolled violence, and to become self-protective at the expense of others.

We must be careful, however, not to gloss over this insight on the spiritual danger of anger. Simeon the New Theologian believed that we can gain control of anger by repentance.[7] When we confront our hostility before God, we can be transformed by His love and receive the gift of a calm spirit. Spiritual writers agree that a failure to seek God's will alone gives rise to self-centeredness and feelings of anger. These are helpful insights for our spiritual growth.

While preaching a series of sermons in a Texas church, I couldn't help noticing a young man who sat at the rear of the congregation. He wept all the way through my sermons. After several days I made it a point to talk with him. What he said was genuinely heartwarming,

> I used to be a very rough person. I worked in the oil fields, which is a very rough environment. I used to fight at the drop of a hat. I was always mad at something or someone. Even when I played games I

was violent. Once I was playing softball and a runner accidently stepped on my foot as he rounded second base. Immediately I tackled him and we got into a big fight. The reason I wept in church is because God has taken that angry spirit out of me. I am so happy now. My life has been changed.

The Lord had given that young man such a spirit of gentleness that now he wanted only to do God's will. Prayer and praise were times of refreshing for him, filling him with strength and compassion.

A WONDERFUL REALITY

Many people think it impossible to live with a Beatitudes mind-set. We see so much hostility in the world. We experience it every-where—at sporting events, in our homes, behind the wheel of our cars. The possibility of seeking God alone and loving as God loves often seems so remote.

Yet Jesus teaches that the gentle are a wonderful reality in the world. They are the people who delight to bend their wills to the will of God. They go out of their way to avoid conflict. Their chief desire is to be like Him who called them, in unassuming love and acceptance of others.

The Apostle Paul understood Christian life as a vocation, a calling that is graced and gifted by the Father (Ephesians 4:1). As Christians we are called by God to live out His will in the world. We are called to sense our spiritual poverty. We are called to be alarmed at our sins and the sins of the world. We are called to listen attentively to God and do what He says. By living out the implications of our vocation in Christ, we witness to a better way for the world to handle its problems.

✝

A MEDITATION ON PLEASING GOD

I have chosen the way of constancy,
I have molded myself to Your judgments.
I cling to Your instructions. . . .
I run the way of Your commandments.

Psalm 119:31a, 32a

━━━━━━━━━━━━━━━━ ▬▬▬ ━━━━━━━━━━━━━━━━

OBSERVE A TIME OF SILENCE

BEATITUDE

Blessed are the gentle:
they shall have the earth as inheritance.

A THOUGHT FOR MEDITATION

"The believer is often in danger of aiming at and rejoicing in what one might call the more human virtues. Such virtues are boldness, joy, contempt for the world, zeal, self-sacrifice. . . . while the deeper and gentler, the more divine and heavenly graces are scarcely thought of or valued. These virtues are those which Jesus first taught upon earth—because He brought them from heaven—those which are more distinctly connected with His cross and the death of self—poverty of spirit, meekness, humility, lowliness. Therefore, let us put on a heart of compassion, kindness, humility, meekness, long-suffering."

Andrew Murray[8]

OBSERVE A TIME OF PRAYER

CLOSING READING

1 Peter 1:3-4

━━━━━━━━━━━━━━━━ ▬▬▬ ━━━━━━━━━━━━━━━━

FIVE

LOOKING FOR LIFE

*B*lessed are those who hunger and
thirst for uprightness:
they shall have their fill.

The passion to experience God was contagious in the early church.
By the middle of the third century A.D., large numbers of Christian
men and women were leaving the cities and fleeing to the desert.
Convinced that their cultural environment was threatening their
attempts to live for God, many became monks, living in small
communes or alone as hermits. It was the beginning of an incredi-
ble lay movement which would not weaken in intensity until the
beginning of the fifth century. These seekers for God had one aim:
to save their souls and grow in the spiritual knowledge of God. In
many ways, theirs was a noble age with sterling examples of vital
spirituality.

The desert fathers in particular were noted as wise counsel-
ors or sages, and their sayings were collected for study and meditation. One of the more popular of these spiritual masters was a man
who lived toward the end of the fourth or beginning of the fifth
century, Poemen by name, sometimes also known as The
Shepherd.

A story is told of a brother (a monk) who came to Poemen,
asking the old man for "a word" (of spiritual wisdom).

"As long as the pot is on the fire," Poemen said, "no fly nor
any other animal can get near it; but as soon as it is cold, these
creatures get inside. So it is with the monk; as long as he lives in

spiritual activities, the enemy cannot find a means of overthrowing him."[1]

This was indeed a good word. This story exemplifies the intensity of early Christian spirituality. The spiritual activities Poemen had in mind were disciplines which cultivated vigilance of heart against temptation. These disciplines revolved around intense prayer and silence. In the heart of the faithful believer today, as well as in Poemen's day, prayer and silence are the flames that keep out the devil and his imps. If one slacks in zeal for God, then the enemy comes in like a flood, drowning the soul in selfishness and greed.

Poemen's advice is just as valid today as when he gave it. His concern for living faith reflects Jesus' concern in the fourth Beatitude—hungering and thirsting for uprightness before God. The spiritual life Jesus brings is one of hungering, thirsting, seeking, knocking in order to find. The soul never takes its ease, as did the unwise farmer of the Gospel parable. God is found only as we actively pursue Him. And then when He is found, God slips away ahead of us and we pursue Him in hungering and thirsting for His presence and for an upright life before Him.

SINCERITY OF FAITH

In this fourth Beatitude, Jesus calls us to seek as though we were starving—which in actuality we are—for an upright life in God's presence. This, of course, is nothing really new to us, nor was it new to those people who heard the Lord on the mountainside. The Jews were familiar with God's demands for righteousness. Every Sabbath they were reminded of this when they heard the prophets read in the synagogue.

> I hate, I scorn your festivals,
> I take no pleasure in your solemn assemblies.
> When you bring Me burnt offerings . . .

> your oblations, I do not accept them
> and I do not look at your communion sacrifices
>   of fat cattle.
> Spare Me the din of your chanting,
> Let Me hear none of your strumming on lyres,
> but let justice flow like water,
> and uprightness like a never-failing stream!
>
> Amos 5:21-24

This would be like God saying to us,

> I cannot tolerate your worship services any more.
> Your prayer meetings give Me no pleasure.
> I will not accept the checks you put in
>   the offering plates.
> Deliver Me from your chorus-singing.
> I don't want to hear your organs and pianos.
> I want you to live uprightly!
> I want you to love one another, and I want you
>   to treat your enemies as brothers.
> I want you to care for the poor and oppressed!

To hunger and thirst after uprightness is to purge our lives of hypocrisy. It is to seek for unity of mind and heart in the Gospel. It is to want a "single eye" for God's glory in every aspect of our lives. Too often we go to church as though fulfilling a religious duty. It is easy to pray for the anxieties of the world and then go home, doing nothing about our prayers. It is clear in the sacred text that God constantly seeks to bring together what we separate—sincere prayer and good works.

When the New Testament writer James says, "You must do what the Word tells you and not just listen to it and deceive yourselves" (1:22), he stands in line with the ancient reformers of Israel. Charity and worship are two sides of the same coin. "Pure, unspoilt religion, in the eyes of God our Father, is this: coming to the help of orphans and widows in their hardships, and keeping oneself uncontaminated by the world" (James 1:27).

Sincerity in the life of faith is what Jesus emphasizes in the fourth Beatitude. He says that sincerity of heart is approved by God. Therefore we can see the following emphases in this Beatitude: the truly fulfilled (happy) people are those

> who passionately yearn for God's approval,
> who have an intense hunger and thirst for God
> to make them upright in everything,
> who set their hearts on God's kingdom
> and His saving justice,
> who actively seek uprightness of heart.

These people, Jesus says, will get all they yearn for and more!

At this point in our study of the spirituality of the kingdom of God, we can see how wonderfully Jesus is leading us into the depths of faith. In the first Beatitude the Lord spoke of being poor in spirit, bringing to the forefront our desperate need of God and our inability to help ourselves. Then He taught us to be alarmed over the depth of our sinfulness and the ease with which we fall into temptation and disobedience. He spoke next about listening only to God for instruction in righteousness, and we learned from that to beware of anger. Now Jesus says to us that we should beware of becoming complacent about our spiritual life. We are to seek the Lord day and night, at every possible moment, in every circumstance, for His will to be done in us. When the will of God is done in our lives, we will be filled with prayer, righteousness, and joy. The further we go into these Beatitudes, the more we see that living them requires a life of seeking and finding, and of more seeking and finding.

THE DESIRE TO PLEASE GOD

The deep desire to release ourselves entirely to God and live in naked faith is shared by many people. One of the most intimate and honest expressions of this desire I know is found in the following prayer by Thomas Merton. See how much of this prayer reflects your own inner longings and hopes.

> My Lord God, I have no idea where I am going. I do not see the road ahead of me. I cannot know for certain where it will end. Nor do I really know myself, and the fact that I think I am following Your will does not mean I am actually doing so. But I believe the desire to please You does in fact please You. And I hope I have that desire in all that I am doing. I hope I will never do anything apart from that desire. And I know that if I do this You will lead me by the right road, though I know nothing about it. Therefore I will trust You always though I may seem to be lost and in the shadow of death. I will not fear, for You are ever with me, and You will never leave me to face my perils alone.[2]

In his beautiful and very honest prayer, Merton gives us two cautions for an upright heart. First, he is suspicious of his own motives. He admits he does not know the depths of his heart, that much is hidden from him. However, he will trust to God's love both what he *does* know and what he *does not* know about himself. Merton does not assume he is innocent! Second, he recognizes the mystery of the future. Even though he may have plans, Merton cannot predict with certainty what will actually happen. So he must trust his future to God, always remembering his is a journey of faith.

These cautions are very important for us. It is fair to say that most of us are afraid of knowing ourselves too well. I have invited many people to go with me on weekend retreats emphasizing silence and prayer. Many times people I invite hesitate, or flatly say no, because, as they tell me, they are apprehensive about spending three days in silence and meditation. They are afraid of what will come to the surface during such experiences. These are legitimate fears. There is much in our hearts we would rather not face. But we must trust God enough to look squarely at our own emptiness and sin. Only by doing this can we know both the agony and relief of opening ourselves to God.

The second caution is that of overlooking the present moment in favor of the future. All of us make future plans, but none of us know if they will actually come to pass. We do have the present moment and in a sense the next moment is our future. To turn our lives over to God's providence, to trust that His goodness will be revealed at the appropriate moment in our lives, is to consciously face our illusion of control. At best we have only marginal control of our lives. Yet we waste enormous amounts of energy trying to control what should be given over to the goodness of God. Our future is the same as our present: God. We are living our future if God is at the center of our lives now. If God is not at the center, there is no future for us anyway. Whatever we might hope to achieve apart from Him is pure illusion.

The central thought of Merton's prayer is contained in the phrase, "I believe the desire to please You does in fact please You." Is this accurate? Yes, because our performance is not the ultimate test of authentic faith. We are called to seek an upright heart. In both the personal and social application of faith, it is our intention to make God smile that makes Him smile. Parents know the child's wish to please them is what is important, not the child's ability to do something great and spectacular. Love alone is the issue! God is our heavenly Parent and we rest securely in His love and acceptance. We do not have to earn His love. It is simply there for us.

Merton then says to our Lord, "I trust You always" and "I will not fear." The unknown is a cause of great fear to many people. But we need not fear because God is always at hand. He will lead us by the right road if we place our trust in Him. It is important to come to the place where *we do not always have to know how God is working in our lives.* We can have confidence God is working in us because our lives are hidden with Christ in God. We can believe that God is ever with us and will never leave us to face our perils alone.

Merton's prayer reflects the beauty of the fourth Beatitude. Jesus wants people to hunger and thirst after God in the same way the tired deer eagerly laps up water from the cool stream (Psalm 42:1-2). If we honestly seek God's kingdom as our first priority, God will not mislead us. It is a spiritual truth that we discover God as we seek Him. As one writer said, the secret of never thirsting for God is to be always thirsting for Him. We are never completely satisfied spiritually in this life. God is always in us, yet we do not contain God. God is in our minds and hearts and at the same time is infinitely beyond what we can think about Him. We know Him through love, not through abstract reasoning or by learning concepts about Him.

NO SUBSTITUTE WILL DO

There is only one ultimate reality: God. Part of our spiritual growth is coming to grips with this truth and aligning ourselves with it. God is the origin and goal of all life, since God is life. Because everything created is derived from God, no thing can make us perfectly happy and satisfied. Created as we are for God Himself, no substitute will do, although we often pack our lives with them, and look for happiness in things created rather than in the Creator.

Very religious people must guard against putting methods of prayer, spiritual disciplines of various kinds, even good works in place of naked faith in God. Methods are helpful as long as they remain channels. When methods become the reality, then we are in trouble. Highly liturgical worship services can be very intense experiences of God's presence. But we can also remember and celebrate God's presence when we wake up in the morning, while we are driving to work, when we play with the family in the evening. Structured times for prayer can help us relate meaningfully to God, but the same is true for spontaneous prayers and momentary meditations on God.

To hunger for God's approval is to recognize that other relationships and things in our lives can function as either idols or icons for us. We know what idols are—objects or relationships or activities to which we attribute ultimate meaning. An idol can be a spouse, a child, a job, a possession, literally anything that commands reverence and obedience. A person who would sell his or her soul for power or wealth is an idolator. We all know people who have made idols of their professions, their abilities, their looks. To hunger and thirst for God is to deny reality to idols.

However, objects, relationships, and especially people, can become icons of God's love for us. In the Greek Orthodox tradition of the church, icons are religious paintings which have been done under special guidance and for deeply spiritual reasons. Icons are usually two-dimensional and the painted figures have a detached, mystical look to them. They are not "realistic" since they are intended to be seen through, to the reality of the God they represent. Icons represent some aspect of God's love, and should lead us to adore and praise God.

People can become icons for us when we see God's activity in and through them, or when they become special objects of love and care which we would give to Christ Himself if it were possible. This does not mean people become objects rather than full human selves. It does mean that they put us in remembrance of God and thereby enrich our experience of God.

To align ourselves with God as ultimate reality means that we come to desire God, not for what He can do for us but for who He is in Himself. It is God, not His gifts, that takes on a sense of final meaning for us. This requires a knowledge of ourselves as needy persons, and the awakening of desire for God, a desire which prompts us to seek Him everywhere.

DEAD ENDS IN SPIRITUAL GROWTH

There are many possible dead ends in cultivating spirituality, or hungering and thirsting for God. I want to mention only three here. I have selected these particular dead ends because they would have been known to those who heard the Lord's Sermon on the Mount. They are also well known to us. Each of them is a threat to the experience of God as ultimate Reality in our lives. They seem to be perpetual problems for seekers for God.

†   We have a tendency to forget that God is near, that He cares for us, and that the eye of faith can see God anywhere. When we forget, we begin to think of God as remote, "up there" some-where, and believe that we do things He cannot see and think thoughts He cannot know. Taken to an extreme, some even believe God does not exist at all; or, if He does, that He doesn't care.

This kind of thinking reduces God from ultimate reality to one-among-many, as just another option for our consideration. The first and second commandments were warnings against this way of thinking (Exodus 20:3-6). The first commandment says we are not to set up a rival to God in our hearts. The second commandment says we are not to make images of God and worship them instead of God. Jesus teaches us that God is to have the central place in our hearts. However much we are tempted to think of God as being far from us, or unconcerned about us, we must resist this serious error.

†   A second dead end in spiritual growth is to allow the formalism of worship to kill our drive to know God. The Scripture does not condemn liturgy in itself. We cannot worship without some kind of liturgy, some recognized way of expressing ourselves. But liturgical practices or orders of service are only forms to help us keep in mind the many dimensions of God's saving love. It is when form becomes a substitute for living faith that it is nauseous to God. If our worship leads us to be open to God and to the needs of other people, then we have worshiped in the tradition of Israel and the prophets.

The lesson that there is no substitute for an upright heart was learned the hard way by the church at Laodicea (Revelation 3:14-22). This New Testament church fell under the judgment of God because they had lost their early bridal love for God. In place of a zealous love for the Lord and a passionate longing for justice, the people had apparently become satisfied with just "going to church." The Lord Himself called the Laodiceans to remember that true worship is much more than offering sacrifices in the temple, or than reading responsive readings or singing hymns.

† Finally, sincerity of heart in seeking the Lord is threatened by any form of works/righteousness. By works/righteousness I mean the false idea that we earn our salvation by being good and by doing good to others. This was at the heart of Jesus' tensions with the Pharisees. Over the years since the original giving of the Law, religious leaders had gradually substituted elaborate legal codes for personal righteousness. Jesus taught that fidelity to the Law was no guarantee of salvation, but was an act of gratitude by those who sought to please God.

On this score Jesus said, "Be careful not to parade your uprightness in public to attract attention." In Matthew 6, we see three examples of what He meant.

> Do not make a big show out of giving money to the poor. Give in such a way that only God knows what you are doing.

> Do not make a public spectacle of your prayers in order to impress people. Spend time in solitude so that only God knows the depth of your prayers.

> Do not call attention to your fasts. Go about business as usual, keeping your fast a secret. Since fasting is for God, only God should know.

As Jesus points out, the true treasures are spiritual. Power, influence, admiration, and legalistic moralisms are snares to the soul, but sincerity and the hidden righteousness of the heart are pleasing to the Lord.

FILLED TO THE BRIM

The promise of Jesus for the God-seekers is that they will get what they want and more! If we genuinely want to please God, that is what the Lord will give us. If we desire to love God, our hearts will fill up with love. Henry Scougal, a seventeenth-century spiritual writer, captures something of the sheer joy of a life that hungers and thirsts for God. Writing of God's presence with us, Scougal says,

> . . . . oh how happy are those who have placed their
> love on Him who can never be absent from them!
> They need but open their eyes, and they shall every-
> where behold the traces of His presence and glory,
> and converse with Him whom their soul loveth. And
> this makes the darkest prison or the wildest desert,
> not only supportable, but delightful to them.
>   [Christians] never think themselves so happy
> as when, having retired from the world, and gotten
> free from the noise and hurry of affairs, and silenced
> all their clamorous passions (those troublesome guests
> within), they have placed themselves in the presence
> of God, and entertain fellowship and communion
> with Him. They delight to adore His perfections, and
> recount His favors, and to protest their affection to
> Him, and tell Him a thousand times that they love
> Him. . . .[3]

Many of the people Jesus spoke to were hungry, thirsty, and tired. Jesus knew how important food, drink, and rest were to them. On a spiritual level, the food and drink of God are necessary for us to live. The heavenly food in the Beatitudes is rich in nourishment. These sayings of Jesus grow human spirits that are happy in the knowledge that all they want is to seek out the living waters and drink. Whoever lives with God in the Beatitudes will know what Paul speaks of when he writes:

> Be filled with the Spirit. Sing psalms and hymns and inspired songs among yourselves, singing and chanting to the Lord in your hearts, always and everywhere giving thanks to God who is our Father in the name of our Lord Jesus Christ.
>
> Ephesians 5:18-20

✝

A MEDITATION ON SEEKING GOD

Blessed be the name of Yahweh,
henceforth and forever.
From the rising of the sun to its setting,
praised be the name of Yahweh!

Psalm 113:2-3

OBSERVE A TIME OF SILENCE

BEATITUDE

Blessed are those who hunger and thirst for uprightness:
they shall have their fill.

A THOUGHT FOR MEDITATION

"O God, the truth, make me one with You in never-dying love. I am so often wearied in reading and hearing many things. In You is all I wish for and desire. Let all who teach fall silent, let all things created remain speechless before You. Do You alone speak to me."

Thomas à Kempis[4]

Committing our cares to God, let us place ourselves before God in silence, seeking Him whom our soul desires.

OBSERVE A TIME OF PRAYER

CLOSING READING

1 John 4:7-13

SIX

LOVING THE LIVING GOD

> "**M**aster, which is the greatest
> commandment of the Law?"
> Jesus said to him, "You must
> love the Lord your God with all your
> heart, with all your soul, and with all
> your mind."   Matthew 22:35-37

The first four Beatitudes of Jesus tell us how to relate to God. Instead of pious platitudes, they are strong words of conflict and struggle. Even on the surface the Beatitudes seem contradictory to what we think we really need.

† Happy are the poor in spirit, those who have no resources left—those who are on rock bottom! Where, I ask you, is the self-assured, upwardly mobile type in these words? Where is the person who knows what he or she wants—the person who has it all together? Where is the well-rounded personality—the take-charge person who is in control of life? Not here. Happy are those who have had the rug yanked out from under them, who land flat on their face. Dance and whoop it up, you who are miserable with yourselves, who are loaded down with guilt, who have a sorry self-image. Give us a big smile, those of you who have been dealt hard blows by life.

† Happy are those who mourn over their sins and the sins of other people. Some respond, "What is this?" Mourners are not

happy; they are sad. They wail, beat their chest in agony, throw dust in the air in despair. True mourners think their world has come to an abrupt stop! This is not the good life. How can we blossom into carefree people if we are burdened with a sin-fixation? What is all this talk of death? We are getting ready to go to the beach. Must we be condemned to always looking over our shoulder for the creeping, devouring lion? Do not disturb us with thoughts of a hidden God, of dark nights of the soul, of the certainty of death. Away with notions like self-denial, cross-bearing, and patience in the face of opposition and pain. We were made to be free!

† Happy are those who listen attentively to God. Now this seems more like it. We are finally getting somewhere. Listen to the soothing voice of God's grace—the tender melody of love. But what are these other words?—words which slay us, words of warning about being too involved in society, words against getting too comfortable with things, words about fasting and prolonged prayer? Why are there sometimes no words? Why is there no answer from the sky about my pain? What do you mean about being called to faith beyond words, beyond explanation, sitting in silence listening to the no-voice of God? Are the no-words of God bread for me as much as the written words?

† Happy are those who yearn passionately for God's approval. As reasonable people, we of course want God's blessing, and we ask for it at mealtime, football games, worship services. God's approval must certainly be on us—good citizens and card-carrying members of the church that we are. . . . we who have a common language, who look and think and act alike. Doesn't God approve of sameness? Why these ideas about placing God above the national interest? About loving God more than parent, spouse, child? What is this stuff about being fools for Christ, about loyalty to God to the point of civil disobedience? Why be wary of receiving awards, commendations, recognition, slaps on the back from an alien people? It's nice to be seen with the right people, to

be able to drop names when necessary. Religion must not go to our heads or make us fanatics!

GOD IN THE BEATITUDES

Notice that the God of the Beatitudes is the One we beg for forgiveness, fear because of His displeasure of sin, listen to as though His were the only voice in the universe, and whose approval we desire more than the approval of anyone else.

God as revealed in the first four Beatitudes is an awesome Sovereign who loves. He strikes terror and gives grace. He is a majestic King, brooking no rivals, and the Father and Lover of the distraught and dispossessed. These Beatitudes are full of struggle and decision-making.

At the same time we see images of acceptance, concern, redemption, and justice. It is God who calls the unjust and sin-sick to Himself. He takes the initiative in the redemption process. God willingly exposes Himself to misunderstanding and rejection in order to redeem us. God is the giver of good gifts: the kingdom, deliverance from sin, grace, and the fulfillment of our desires which have Him as their end. God is happy, as the word is used in the Beatitudes, and shares His happiness with those of us who want it.

God does not present Himself to us in the Beatitudes under only one or two forms. His nature is varied and complex. Often the images seem to cancel each other—how can God be both judge and lover? On the one hand, God is very close, interacting with us on the most intimate levels. On the other, God is remote, transcendent, fixing a great gulf between Him and His creatures. Both of these images are needed to gain a proper perspective on God, but neither is totally true, if taken to an extreme.

The Prophet Isaiah would have understood Jesus perfectly, since many of these images of God merge in the vision Isaiah had in the temple, shortly after the death of the king (Isaiah 6). In his vision of the Holy One in His war counsel chambers, Isaiah saw the glory of God on a throne of majesty and judgment. The form of God, however, was no reduction of Divinity since there was no face to describe! Isaiah could only see a vague form, without detail. This God is not William Blake's "Ancient of Days," a divine figure, nude and old, with flowing beard and hair in the rushing wind, kneeling to throw lightning bolts from his fingers at the earth. The true God is the unspeakable, indescribable reality who is feared, sought, listened to, yielded to, obeyed, but never questioned. Though there are no words of graciousness in the sixth chapter of Isaiah, still the grace of God surrounds the event, since God is jealous for the work of His saving Word among the people.

The Pharisees of Jesus' day could not understand the God of the Beatitudes, even though they stood in Isaiah's tradition. Their ancestors had reduced God to a set of formal laws and the Pharisees perpetuated their error. Attitudes of the heart seemed to be of secondary concern. The Lord called them hypocrites because of their refusal to see what God was doing through Christ. To the Pharisees, God was a legalistic deity, who could more readily be satisfied with codes written on parchment than with codes written on the heart.

But the Pharisees were saints when compared with some representatives of evangelical Christianity today. For many, God seems to be a cosmic bellboy, whose sole business is to guarantee His children a good life. They apparently think God can be manipulated with money. I heard a TV evangelist tell listeners that an "advance tithe" sent in on monies they need would in turn "obligate" the Lord to give them what they asked. Do you need a thousand dollars? Send in one hundred and God is "obligated" to send you the thousand! What would Isaiah or Jesus have done with this idea? God cannot be controlled by human beings. To think so is the essence of magic, which is condemned in Scripture.

The true God is clothed with mystery. To the repentant and the seekers this mystery can be warmth and goodness, but it remains mystery nonetheless. The notion that we can command

God to do what we want is guaranteed to cause spiritual casualties, leaving weak believers scattered far and wide, because they have gone through the motions and the skies are silent, they think they have been betrayed, and they lose heart.

The God of the Beatitudes was the God of a professional boxer whom I saw being interviewed on television. He was going into the ring in a matter of minutes. It was a title fight and very important to his career. "This is a crucial fight for you," the announcer said. "How do you feel going into it?" "Win or lose," he said, "I praise the name of Jesus Christ."

This is it! The God of the Beatitudes reveals Himself once more. God can be trusted to work on our behalf, regardless of the circumstances. Our response to the justice and love of God is one of grateful submission and confidence. Happiness is for those who are committed to the God of Jesus, win or lose. In light of the truth that God is our final destiny, nothing else is of utmost importance. The Beatitudes tell of winning, but in God's time and according to God's purpose. They tell of a God who is for us!

THE FIRST FOUR BEATITUDES: A PARAPHRASE

All of the Beatitudes we have discussed so far have a common theme: *those who eagerly seek God are truly happy*. Because God had us in mind from before the creation of the world, He now wants to help us become what He wanted us to be in the first place. This means that spiritual life is not to be thought of as something strange or artificial, imposed on real life. To walk consciously with God is real life. Neither is spirituality simply a new set of rules we reluctantly accept, something like a bit in a horse's mouth. True life, which is true spirituality, is to love God for His own sake, that is, simply because He is, and because He is love. A spiritual life is therefore a joyous life. Authentic spirituality leads us naturally into a life of "beauty, loveliness, and integrity."[1]

I think the root meaning of the first four Beatitudes can be seen in the following paraphrase.

> How deeply happy are those who recognize their need of God: God's kingdom belongs to them!

> And joyous are those who are alarmed because of sin: God will rescue them from it!

> Inwardly content are those who listen attentively to God: They will receive as a gift what belongs to God!

> Truly fulfilled are those who really want to live an upright life: They will get their heart's desire!

When you and I sincerely allow the Holy Spirit to shape our lives according to these teachings of Jesus, we will come to know what it means to love God with all our heart, mind, soul, and strength.

Seen from one perspective, the first four Beatitudes represent progressive steps or stages of intimacy with God. From another perspective, they are continuing attitudes through which we understand our ongoing relationship with the Father. Therefore we can see the meaning of these Beatitudes in the following ways.

† Recognizing our need of God is the first step toward the kingdom. As we continue to recognize our need of God we are kept by the Spirit from becoming arrogant in our faith, from making demands on others, and from judging them.

† Being alarmed because of sin makes us aware of the depth of God's love for us. Continued awareness of sin, ours and that of others, helps us remember God's mercy and gentleness toward the undeserving.

† Listening attentively to God alone causes us to abandon all hope of salvation apart from God's grace. As we continue to listen attentively to God, we develop an appreciation for meditation and prayer, and the desire to do God's will above all else.

† Wanting with all our hearts to live an upright life before God is a natural desire if we live in the light of the first three Beatitudes. A continuing desire for God's approval helps us think and act in ways that please God, ways we learn from the Bible, through prayer, and in consultation with spiritual friends.

NURTURING LOVE FOR GOD

Our love for God can grow in many directions. As we will see in the Beatitudes to come, we deepen our relationship with God whenever we act in ways that help other people. Adoration and love are also increased by meditating on Scripture, reading devotional literature, conversing with friends about the love of God, participating in acts of worship, receiving Holy Communion. For those who have eyes to see, nature may reflect the love and care of God. It is also possible to detect the love of God in times of our deepest sorrow.

Whenever we find God's love at work, it is natural for our love to go back to God. But of all the means we have of saying "I love You" to God, none is as rich in meaning as prayer. Prayer is a living interaction with God. Sometimes prayer is talking to God; sometimes it is an unrushed listening. Prayer is much more than asking for things, for it attempts to experience God's presence in a sense of relationship and shared interest. Prayer is exploring God, talking with Him, listening to Him, reflecting on what He means to us.

Most of our prayer experiences will have two dimensions to them: open, free exchange with God as our Father; and silent awareness of God's presence, or at least our desire for that presence.

When our relationship with God is living and vital, prayer is more a matter of the heart than of the mind. One spiritual teacher described *prayer as a continual standing before God with the mind in the heart.* This is an excellent figure of speech. It means *we are called to love God, rather than figure Him out.* Picking up on this notion of the heartfelt nature of prayer, Carlo Carretto writes:

> So true prayer demands that we be more passive than active; it requires more silence than words, more adoration than study, more concentration than rushing about, more faith than reason. . . .

> True prayer is a gift from heaven to earth, from the Father to His child, from the Bridegroom to the bride, from He who has to him who has not, from Everything to nothing.[2]

For me, the key ingredient is to relate to God as He is, a living, loving Presence. God is always with us and He is responsive to overtures of love, expressions of gratitude, and moments of admiration. However, just as healthy marriages require times for serious talking and reflecting, so we need intentional times for prayer as well. A very busy friend of mine makes appointments with God. When the time comes for that appointment, he tells his secretary that he is not to be interrupted, just as he would not want to be interrupted with an important client.

Because of our mood swings, there are times when it is easy to talk with our spouse or a close friend, and times when it is more difficult. We experience the same thing with God—there are times when God is so close we think we will burst with His sensed presence. There are other times when we think God has gone on vacation without telling us. Do not be concerned about this absence of God, unless you know it was caused by your disobedience which calls for repentance and restoration. Otherwise, if your prayers seem dry and dull, do not worry. God hears and cares. Be patient and wait for God; do not feel depressed, thinking God has abandoned you during such times. He may be trying to pull you into the depths of yourself in order to teach you how much you need Him.

Prayer is a means to an end, but not the end, no more than

the act of talking is an end in itself. There are no magic words, or chants, or methods. God is the object of our prayers, not the particular method we use. This is not to say that methods are not helpful or desirable. We can often gain tremendous insight into prayer by using certain forms for a time. There are a variety of methods in the books suggested at the end of this book. But the day will come for those who walk with God, when our methods are set aside in favor of the constant flow of communication between our souls and God.

What could be better than this?

THE JOY OF LOVING GOD

Thomas Kelly, a Quaker mystic, shares what happens when God's love breaks in on us, making "life glorious and new"!

> One sings inexpressibly sweet songs within oneself,
> and one *tries* to keep one's inner hilarity and exuber-
> ance within bounds lest, like the men of Pentecost,
> we be mistaken for men filled with new wine. [3]

What Kelly calls *exuberance* and some Christians call *ecstasy* is a deep, extremely personal joy which flows from our hearts when God expresses His presence to us in ways we understand. It is like the flush of love we felt the first time we said to our mate, "I love you." It is the sense of unbridled excitement a young child experiences on being given a beautifully wrapped gift. It is the joy of the Lord, the gift of the Spirit. Thank God this joy comes and goes, for we could not stand the constant bubbling up of waves of pleasure and happiness that loving God often brings.

The first four Beatitudes help us to develop a lasting and intimate relationship with God as Father. Such love must necessarily spill over on people we associate with—family members and friends. It is impossible to bottle up the enthusiasm of the Spirit and keep it as though it were a private gift. We must share, even though sometimes that sharing is costly. It is to this aspect of kingdom spirituality that we now give our attention as we look at the last four Beatitudes.

✝

A MEDITATION ON PRAYER

Yahweh, my heart is not haughty,
I do not set my sights too high.
I have taken no part in great affairs,
in wonders beyond my scope.
No, I hold myself in quiet and silence,
like a little child in its mother's arms,
like a little child, so I keep myself.
Let Israel hope in Yahweh
henceforth and for ever.   Psalm 131

OBSERVE A TIME OF SILENCE

BEATITUDE

How blessed are all those who take refuge in Him!   Psalm 2:12

A THOUGHT FOR MEDITATION

"Genuine prayer is never 'good works,' an exercise or a pious attitude,
but it is always the prayer of a child to a Father."

Dietrich Bonhoeffer[*]

Let us beware of two extremes in prayer: of thinking ourselves so
friendly with God that we forget His majesty, or being so fearful of
God that we forget His desire for intimacy.

OBSERVE A TIME OF PRAYER

CLOSING READING

Matthew 6:7-15

SEVEN

SHARING GOD'S MERCY

*B*lessed are the merciful:
they shall have mercy shown them.

During my university studies, I took a course in criminology. One night our class went to the city jail and from there to a night court. I was deeply moved by the "mercy of the court" as I watched person after person stand before the judge. Most of the charges were misdemeanors, such as vagrancy and loitering. Some of those charged were street people with no place to go, or high schoolers picked up for speeding or disturbing the peace. Many of the defendants were obviously frightened, dreading the possibility of a steep fine or having to spend a few nights locked up. Several times the judge would let the guilty off with a stern lecture and promises that the next time they would get "the book" thrown at them.

The mercy of the court was cold and hard, and humiliating to those receiving it. The tone of the proceedings was businesslike and threatening. As a young Christian, I naturally made connections between what I was seeing and the mercy of God. There seemed to be such a contrast.

On occasion biblical writers used legal terms to express our relationship with God. We are justified by faith, says Paul the Apostle. The word *justify* is a term related to the courts. In terms of salvation, justification is like standing before God as Judge. At this trial your guilt is beyond dispute. Everyone in the courtroom knows it, from the prosecuting attorney to the youngest onlooker. There is no question. It is an open and shut case. You literally have no defense. There is no way out.

When the Judge calls you to the bench, you expect the worst. It is only fitting, though you hate to admit it. But unexpectedly the Judge says you are free to go. Guilty, you are set free! Not only are the just charges against you dropped, but the record is clean. It is as though you were never arrested in the first place. To make matters more baffling, everyone in the courtroom is happy, especially the Judge! Everyone is cheering, and the Judge embraces you. He couldn't wait to pronounce you guiltless. Instead of the humiliation which you felt, you are happy beyond belief. This is God's "mercy of the court."

To arrive at the spiritual awareness that we have really received mercy from God is truly a "crisis" moment. It is a devastating experience to stand exposed before God, to have nothing to say for ourselves. It is the moment when we are found out, when the mask has been ripped off. It is to stand before God covered with nothing but the illusions of our past, illusions that dissolve and give us no relief. It is like the prodigal son waking up in the pig pen, stuffing his gnawing body with dry husks. It is to return home in shame and disgust to be met by a waiting Father who smothers His child with love instead of judgment. Here is the crisis: we who do not deserve to be loved are loved by an infinite Love! This is mercy indeed. This is why baptisms are such joyful occasions.

When we are baptized, we are confirmed in the grace of God, a grace that radically changes all of life. In every branch of the church, the act of baptism is a line of demarcation; it represents a crossing over from one life to another, from the kingdom of darkness to the kingdom of light. To be baptized in the name of Jesus Christ is always understood as a conformity of our lives to His life. The rite of baptism is the sign of God's mercy meeting our needs head-on with triumph!

Baptism gives us a name: Christian! Baptism indicates new life: resurrection! In baptism we turn from the world: renunciation! Baptism is a sign and seal of our relationship with Christ: salvation! Baptism is a pledge to live according to Christ's teaching: obedience! Our daily life in Christ is nothing else than putting into practice the implication of baptism. Therefore, God's mercy is the heart of Christian baptism.

HAVING MERCY ON EVERYONE

This Beatitude declares that we are happy when our mercy knows no bounds. When we are merciful we are doing what God does, for He is patient and kind to everyone, even those who flaunt His will. God is long-suffering, the Scripture says; that is, God deliberately withholds His righteous judgment in order that many of those who resist Him will come to their senses and turn to Him for mercy. God is mercy because God is love.

Those who heard Jesus preach on the mountainside thought of God's mercy in terms of His covenant with the Israelites. Whenever the Jews worshiped, they were reminded that their tradition reflected God's goodness to them. That the Creator God should choose them—originally a tiny tribe of nomads—to be His witnesses among the nations was always a cause for wonder and celebration. The following verses are praises for God's mercy and faithfulness to the tiny chosen nation.

> Alleluia!
> Give thanks to Yahweh, call on His name,
> proclaim His deeds to the peoples!
>
> Sing to Him, make music for Him,
> recount all His wonders!
> Glory in His holy name,
> let the hearts that seek Yahweh rejoice! . . .
>
> Stock of Abraham, His servant,
> Children of Jacob whom He chose!
> He is Yahweh our God;
> His judgments touch the whole world.

He remembers His covenant for ever,
the promise He laid down for a thousand
    generations,
which He concluded with Abraham,
the oath He swore to Isaac.

                                    Psalm 105: 1-3, 6-9

Since God is merciful by nature, the people were expected
to be merciful by grace. The Hebrews were people living in a
covenant relationship to God. The most famous covenant was the
Ten Commandments, a document which gave the people an identity (Exodus 20: 1-17). The Commandments became the marks of
God's mercy shown to a particular people, and through them to all
the world.

As the Hebrews gradually lost confidence in the covenant
and turned to the gods of their neighbors, they suffered military
defeats at the hands of foreign powers. The people despaired and
often turned a deaf ear to the prophets.

Then, in the fullness of time, the mercy of God surfaced in
a marvelous way. Listen to its echoes in a virgin's song.

My soul proclaims the greatness of the Lord
and my spirit rejoices in God my Saviour,
because He has looked upon the humiliation
of His servant. . . .

Holy is His name,
and His faithful love extends age after age
to those who fear him.

Mary sang of God's mercy in remembering His covenant of
old times. The Lord God was already at work in her, the virgin,
fulfilling ancient prophecies. The Almighty was beginning to rout
the arrogant, dethrone wicked rulers, raise up the lowly, fill the
starving with good foods, and send the greedy rich away empty

handed. The dawn of redemption was at hand.

At last the Father was coming to the aid of His beaten people, recalling His pledge of faithful love. The Lord had not totally forgotten His mercy to Abraham and his descendants. Mary's wonderful song of mercy deserves to be called The Magnificat. The Son of Mary was to exemplify personal and social redemption in a manner unparalleled in human history (Luke 1:46-55).

THE CENTER OF ALL MERCY

God's mercy can be seen. There are many examples of this, particularly in the Old Testament. By the time of Jesus, every Hebrew child knew by heart the story of the two greatest acts of divine mercy in the history of the Jewish people: the deliverance at the Red Sea (Exodus 14:15-31) and the miraculous return of the Hebrew exiles from captivity (in Ezra and Nehemiah). These two marvelous events became the subjects of prayers, songs, and praises. But as powerful as these images of love were for the people, the most outstanding was still to come.

> Indeed, there is but one center of all mercy, one merciful event, in which we receive mercy and give it. . . . This event is the saving mystery of the Cross, which alone enables us to enter into a true spiritual harmony with one another, seeing one another not only in natural fellowship but in the Spirit and mercy of Christ, who emptied Himself and became obedient to death. . . .'

On the cross of our Lord Jesus, God the Father entered into the deepest pain of our anxiety and sin. In this one supreme act, God forever showed Himself as Mystery consumed by lowliness and love. God Incarnate stood before false accusers that He might have mercy on our duplicity and self-justification. The Mighty One endured the humiliation of cruel beatings and mockery so that He might have mercy on our violent and destructive selves. The Majestic One was nailed in agony and shame to one of His creatures, a tree, that He might have mercy on our insolence. The Eternal One died one midafternoon that He might rescue us, the unlovely and undeserving, from eternal night.

We stand transfixed before the cross, mute, condemned by our grasping powerlessness, cowardice, and fear. Blatant sinners howl and jeer, as their hearts harden like steel against their own internal struggles. They wag their heads, gamble for His clothing, turn away from His sacrifice as they wonder about their investments. All the while mercy flows in blood and sweat while human beings, made in the image of God, crush that image into the dust through unfair competition, manipulation of the poor, apathy in the face of death, and the horror of war. Those, however, who open their eyes to see Him nailed there for them will be forever changed by the kind cross of a merciful Saviour.

The world today survives by virtue of the crucifixion, which demonstrates the patience and agony of God's self-giving. Take away the cross and resurrection of Jesus and the world will be left with only human ingenuity motivated by self-interest. The cross comes to us as both judgment and mercy. It is judgment in that it calls into question our preoccupation with profits and ease. It is mercy because it brings us near to God who enables us to live in ways that please Him.

The cross of Jesus is our place of reconciliation with one another. It is both the example and the power which can make the human community gracious and kind. The cross shows us how to absorb personal and cultural shocks without fighting back. The cross teaches us to truly forgive, returning good for evil. The cross frees us of self-seeking so that we may be genuinely self-giving.

One must often give up personal rights in order to be merciful to the vulgar and the hostile. Feelings of hatred and vengeance must be set aside for the good of the rebellious. This is why the Eucharist, the "giving thanks" commonly referred to as the

Lord's Supper, is the church's primary symbol of divine humiliation and mercy. In the Eucharist, time stands still, as we are faced again with the Lord as a wounded lover. We go from this high celebration of God's grace with His own power. This power works mightily in us to enable us to live selfless lives for the good of all.

THE PAIN OF MERCY

The cross shows us that the grace of mercy is terribly costly. Christ extends mercy to the pitiful, the unthankful, and the resentful. We are called to do the same. It is naturally easier to have mercy on those who appreciate it, pity toward people who do not grab whatever they can and run. Compassion flows more naturally to those who suffer than to those who cause suffering.

The Holy Spirit teaches us early in our walk with Christ that we do not deserve the mercy we receive from God. But it is because we did receive mercy while we were sinners that we are now freed to extend it to whoever needs it. Whether our mercy will change the rebellious is not the issue. The issue is purely one of need. You see, God is making us like Himself. It should not surprise us, though it may confuse some who know us, to find that we increasingly prefer patience to swift retaliation, loving acts to threats of violence, and a desire for peace instead of the desire to wage war. All we need do is look at Jesus' life to find that there are no limits to His love and mercy.

Giving mercy is not easy because we are almost sure to be misunderstood by someone. It takes great discernment to know how to be a merciful Christian. I often find that the Lord awakens my conscience on the subject of mercy and then lets me struggle with how it is to be applied.

Some years ago I traveled with a Christian witness team from Los Angeles to Phoenix, Arizona. The car in which I rode was driven by a sergeant on the Los Angeles police force. He was a witty and talkative man, deeply concerned that his faith in Christ shape his life as a policeman. As we talked, it became clear he was having a tough time of it. There were several youth gangs in his precinct and he was having difficulty relating to them.

"I really try to show those gang members that I love them," he said. "But all I seem to be doing is losing their respect. They respond to power, not love. If I am rough with them, then they listen. They don't like it, of course, but at least they respect my authority. But if I try to show compassion, they think I am soft and try to walk all over me. What can I do?"

I had no answer for the brother, and I don't think he was really expecting one. I was an outsider and couldn't appreciate the underlying dynamics of his situation. Though he seemed to be in a tight spot, I was convinced that as a disciple of Jesus he was called to love. Through prayer and self-denial, God would reveal to his heart how he was to apply the rule of justice and mercy.

MERCY: THE GOOD MEASURE

Be merciful, just as your Father is merciful. Do not judge, and you will not be judged. Do not condemn, and you will not be condemned. Forgive, and you will be forgiven. Give, and it will be given to you. A good measure, pressed down, shaken together and running over, will be poured into your lap. For with the measure you use, it will be measured to you.

Luke 6:36, 38, NIV

Mercy freely given can counter anger and fear because the merciful person affirms the worth of the person receiving mercy. Mercy says, "I understand you and what you are feeling." Mercy says, "I offer you what I would like to have if I were in your circumstances." In spite of this, mercy is sometimes rejected. The reason may be simply that the receiver does not understand what the giver is doing. It may be that mercy is suspect because it is taken to be an act of superiority. However, persistent, loving attention and self-giving is hard to resist, and may at last be seen for what it is—free grace given from a broken heart now mended.

What does the Lord mean by saying that God gives mercy to the merciful? The first four Beatitudes all have divine mercy as their foundation. Perhaps God gives mercy to those who want more than anything else to do what pleases God. This mercy may be in the form of spiritual discernment, spiritual knowledge of God, assurance of relationship with God, the sense of God's fullness in our hearts, or deeper and more meaningful prayer. This mercy gives us patience in trials, the grace to see things as they really are, or the fire and light in one's heart, burning in love for God.

Mercy has the capacity to establish relationships. Mercy is going the second mile to preserve peace. As God draws us into His mercy, to live there and relate to Him as servant to master, slave to king, child to parent—and to desire it to be that way—so our spirit of mercy can bond enemies together in the light of love. Such mercy produces peace and a feeling of self-worth.

Mercy is a "good measure" when it enables us to see Christ more clearly. You and I must live by faith, but if we keep our eyes open we just may occasionally see the Lord. Mother Teresa has discovered one way of doing this. At her children's home in Calcutta, her sisters offer a daily prayer asking that they be permitted to see Jesus in the sick and dying.

> Dearest Lord,
> May I see You today and every day in the person of Your sick, and whilst nursing them, minister to You. Though You hide yourself behind the unattractive disguise of the irritable, the exacting, the unreasonable, may I still recognize You, and say: "Jesus, my Patient, how sweet it is to serve You." Lord, give me this seeing faith; then my work will never be monotonous. [2]

Another blessing of mercy is in the release it brings from having to be noticed and applauded. Genuine mercy loves for God to be recognized. It is God alone who is the fountain of mercy. And since we have received mercy, we no longer have to continually justify ourselves. We can simply live with ourselves in God's mercy. All of this means that mercy can free us from the sometimes damaging effects of the admiration of others.

Finally, Jesus' teaching points out that His life in us is made possible only through grace. That in itself is a great blessing. We are enabled by God's power to do what we otherwise would not be able to do at all. Recently on the nightly news a woman was commenting on a reprieve being sought by a death-row inmate. She reminded the reporter that the inmate had killed "without mercy." Then she asked, "Why should we have mercy on him?" His crimes had certainly been horrible, and public justice required that he be punished for them. Mercy cannot automatically cancel out the consequences of vicious acts. But mercy does dictate our attitude toward such miserable people. The spirit of mercy is not vengeful. We can live free of hatred toward others. What if God had said of us, "Why should I have mercy on them?" We know God's mercy is surely the "good measure!"

What life is richer, more satisfying, than this? It cannot be had for money, because it would be a poor trade to gain the world and lose our soul in the process (Luke 9:25). What life is more noble than that lived with genuine pity and affection for those whose lives are torn apart by circumstances or evil motives? What individual is more admirable than one eager to sacrifice everything in order to hear God's approval? To live for mercy is to live for love. To give mercy freely is to shatter the power of selfishness and set in motion the momentum of a life genuinely free!

✝

A MEDITATION ON SHOWING MERCY

He has shown you, O man, what is good.
And what does the Lord require of you?
To act justly and to love mercy
and to walk humbly with your God.

Micah 6:8, NIV

OBSERVE A TIME OF SILENCE

BEATITUDE

Blessed are the merciful:
They shall have mercy shown them.

A THOUGHT FOR MEDITATION

"Because we cannot see Christ, we cannot express our love to Him; but our neighbors we can always see, and we can do to them what, if we saw Him, we would like to do to Christ."

Mother Teresa of Calcutta[3]

The way of Jesus is to show mercy on others, especially those who deserve it least. If we are not in a position to extend mercy, at least we can refrain from being judgmental. That in itself is a form of mercy.

OBSERVE A TIME OF PRAYER

CLOSING READING

Matthew 20:20-34

EIGHT

IMPROVING SPIRITUAL VISION

*B*lessed are the pure in heart:
they shall see God.

In his fine book of poems for children, Shel Silverstein makes a plea
for the restoration of our lost innocence.

> I will not play at tug o' war.
> I'd rather play at hug o' war,
> Where everybody hugs
> Instead of tugs.
> Where everyone giggles
> And rolls on the rug,
> Where everyone kisses,
> And everyone grins,
> And everyone cuddles,
> And everyone wins.[1]

This spirit of Camelot, this paradise regained, is strikingly
close to Jesus' words about purity of heart. In each of us is the hope
that love and innocence can really come to dominate our lives.
Every baby represents purity, and there is always a sense of outrage
at the child molester and the child pornographer because they
crush our hopes for a better world, a world of hug o' war.

But Silverstein's dream seems so remote, so impossible.
Social critics of our time, in the arts and in politics, bemoan our
tendency to suspicion, party spirit, and the desire to wage war. In
our own country's history we see something of this preoccupation

with fearful, destructive behavior. In the twentieth century we have moved from easy optimism at the turn of the century to a sordid pessimism as we near its end. At first we placed our hopes in the philosophy of progress, a confidence which seemed justified by technological advance and the rise of modern medicine. But with this child Progress, a twin was born that was the opposite of everything good, beautiful, and true. That demonic twin manifested itself in death camps, atomic bombs, and terrorism. Against our deepest longings we have made French playright Eugene Ionesco a prophet, believing as he does that human nature seeks first to destroy others and failing that destroys itself.

And yet to us today, Jesus still speaks the unbelievable words, "Blessed are the pure in heart."

THE VOCATION OF THE CHURCH

Recently I was with a group of students visiting a local Roman Catholic monastery. Most of the students had never been inside a monastery and were quite taken by what they saw. We had an opportunity to talk with one of the monks of the community and ask questions about their life. One of the students asked rather point-blank what those monks were doing there in the first place. The old man thought for a moment. There were many ways he could have answered the student's question. But instead of appealing to the Bible or to the history of the church, he simply said, "There ought to be a place where people can live together and love one another."

It is the calling of the people of God to fulfill that monk's longing—to live together in love and do the will of God. But what is the will of God for the loving community and how does that relate to purity of heart? To answer this we must go back to the Old Testament, where we discover the mind-set of the people who heard the Lord speak on the mountain.

A major theme in the Old Testament is the unique role that

Israel was to play in relation to other nations. The distinctive character of that role is seen in the covenant God made with Abraham. This covenant promised to make Abraham a "great nation" for the specific purpose of blessing "all the clans of the earth" (Genesis 12:3). This distinctive call remained on the house of Israel through succeeding ages (Exodus 19:5). In being a blessing to the other nations, Israel was to perform two tasks: to function as priests, bringing the people's needs before God; and to function as prophets, bringing God's Word to the nations.

Israel was to be a "light to the Gentiles" (Isaiah 42:6). That meant the holy nation would be a servant to other people and to God. As with Camelot, however, this plan was never really put into effect. As time passed Israel became an adversary of its neighbors, though this was not always Israel's fault. A covenant written on paper for all to read proved inadequate, but God's will could not be frustrated by disobedience. It was the Prophet Jeremiah who foresaw a new work God would do—He would write the covenant not on parchment but on the hearts of His people (31:31-34).

Jesus' announcement that God wanted a people with pure hearts raised hopes that once again Israel would become a "light to the Gentiles." We now know the words of Jesus were to inspire the church—the called-out ones—to continue their praying /prophesying role (Titus 2:11-14; 1 Peter 2:9). According to God's will, the church was to become the new Israel. To be purified meant that the church was to see itself set aside for a unique destiny. And since the church is a universal reality, anyone can become a servant to others in the church. Therefore the church becomes the servant community and every person is invited to become part of it. The church is called to be pure in heart.

This Beatitude about purity of heart is not fantasy, but a reaffirmation of the will of God. There is a certain simplicity of desire and goal in the church's teaching. This simplicity manifests itself in the intercession of the church for the rest of the world, coupled with the church's announcement that the will of God can be accomplished in and through Jesus Christ. It is of the utmost necessity that the church gain purity of heart—that is, follow the call of God with single-minded devotion, and marshal all its energies for sacrificial love.

INNER RIGHTEOUSNESS

Purity of heart not only means obedience to the will of God as far as the church's vocation as a whole is concerned; it also means a radical change in our hearts individually. A pure heart is a heart redirected toward the love of God and neighbor. It is uncluttered in its adoration of God and has a single-minded desire to do His will in everything. This sense of direction is an inner reality, welling up from inside. In fact, the love of God becomes so real that it completely overlooks trivial matters such as denominational differences in the church, or varying views of worship. Purity of heart is a foundation for the unity of all Christians in Christ.

The opposite of purity of heart is the spirit of Pharisaism. For all their good qualities, and there were many, the Pharisees were blatant legalists. Their devotion to God and their service to others were cluttered with laws, through which they lost their simple love. And as a result of their theological hardheadedness, the Pharisees were a constant thorn in the side of Christ. Jesus called the Pharisees "hypocrites" because they piled unnecessary legalistic burdens on the people (Matthew 23:13-32). Of course, many people like a legalistic faith that helps them measure their responses to God, thinking they can avoid the way of naked faith.

All of us have known such Christians. They mean well; however, their insistence on being right or having some special insight often results in a warped view of faith. I encountered one of them just after I was called into Christian ministry. As a recent convert, I really did not know much about the faith. I knew something wonderful had happened in my life, that Jesus Christ had brought meaning and forgiveness to me. In my ignorance I thought Christians all believed pretty much the same thing. I was not prepared for the competition and in-fighting I was later to see in the church.

One afternoon when I was browsing in a Christian bookstore, a clerk I knew called me over.

"See that young man over there?" she asked, pointing to a fellow a few aisles over.

"Yes," I answered.

"Well, he is going to be a minister too, and I thought you might want to meet him."

I thanked her and walked over to the young man who was thumbing through a book. As I approached he looked up. I stuck out my hand and introduced myself. I told him I was planning on being a minister too.

He looked me straight in the eye, knitted up his brow and asked, "Are you a premillenialist?"

My hand was still extended and now my mind was racing. What was a premillenialist? I had never heard of that before. I couldn't even spell it! But it was obvious that my response was very important to him.

"Yes, I am," I shot back.

"Put 'er there!" he said with a big grin.

I was puzzled as we shook hands. I did not know what I had said, so I didn't hang around for conversation, but hurried off to find out what I had become.

I later discovered that premillenialism is one Christian view of what is to happen in the world before the return of our Lord. Premillenialism says Christ will return to earth during times of unbelievable stress and wickedness, and will establish His rule which will last for one thousand years (Revelation 20:1-2). While premillenialism is an important belief to many Christians, not all believers understand events leading up to the end time quite that way.

The point is that my young brother had fallen into the

Pharisee's trap. He was basing our relationship on a debatable point of Christian doctrine rather than on the living faith inside both of us. Since then I have had many similar encounters. Teaching as I do at a confessional theological school—a seminary with a particular theological perspective—I meet many ministers who are convinced that our tradition has all the truth when it comes to knowing God's will. Some of these people continue to drink from the Pharisee's cup, forgetting the sincere search for truth in other Christian traditions. In such instances, purity of heart goes out of the window and the church remains divided. In terms of Jesus' emphasis, true righteousness is more a matter of the heart than following certain prescribed doctrinal formulas.

A PURE INTENTION

Jesus' call to purity of heart is a call to freedom in the Spirit. The truly happy life has a clear aim: to please God in everything. Jesus helps us understand that purity of heart involves "a simple directness in one's intentions and attitudes, an undivided heart, a one-track mind when it comes to the things of God."[2] This is freedom indeed. We do not have to be concerned over details in worship, we simply worship. We do not have to insist that everyone experience the Lord the way we do. No, our one reality is Christ.

Purity of heart is to have a one-track mind with regard to the will of God. Nothing must become a rival to our love for God, even if it is something good. We sometimes have a tendency to let our service for Christ become a substitute for a longing heart to know Him more fully. To be active in missions work is a good thing. But to be so active in missions that one has little or no time to wait before God in prayer is to miss the point of true discipleship. Our first priority is an unhindered, unrushed experience of God, preferably in quietness and solitude. Then we can go from that experience renewed and energized to do the work of the Lord.

This means that a pure heart has one intention: to have

one's will shaped by the will of God. This is one reason why worship is so important to those seeking purity of heart. The worship of God releases love in us, love that goes out to God and therefore loves what God loves. To love God with all one's heart is at the same time to love one's neighbor, because God loves all people. This kind of highly personalized experience shapes the intention of our hearts to do always what delights the Father. Along this line, Thomas Merton says,

> Our intentions are pure when we identify our advantage with God's glory, and see that our happiness consists in doing His will because His will is right and good. In order to make our intentions pure, we do not give up all ideas of seeking our own good, we simply seek it where it can really be found: in a good that is beyond and above ourselves. [3]

THE FREEDOM OF THE HEART

The quest for purity of heart is the root of all spiritual discipline. This quest leads us to meditation and prayer, and it sustains us during times of spiritual struggle. Purity of heart is concerned about relating to the Lord. According to Paul, such singlemindedness is the goal of authentic faith (Colossians 2:6-7).

The quest for purity of heart causes us to always want to do the right thing. This desire should not lead us into an obsessive introspection, always fearful we have done the wrong thing. Rather we are to be open, sensing what is good at the moment, leaning on the leading of the Spirit, following the instructions and meanings of Scripture.

The quest for purity of heart frees us from the grasping influence of the world around us. The pure in heart know they must rest in the Lord, even in the midst of a very busy life. Such devotion to God keeps us from being overly impressed with the values of our society. In effect, purity of intention simplifies our needs and focuses our attention on Christ instead.

The quest for purity of heart makes us aware of the needs of other people. God's love is directed toward redeeming, enhancing, and healing the lives of people. The more our hearts are filled with God, the more we want to identify with the powerless and the underprivileged.

The pure heart is one filled with God. Paul the Apostle knew this simple truth and urged the Philippians to concentrate on God's goodness and blessings.

> Finally . . . let your minds be filled with everything that is true, everything that is honorable, everything that is upright and pure, everything that we love and admire—with whatever is good and praiseworthy. . . . the God of peace will be with you." (4:8-9)

THE PROMISE OF SEEING GOD

The promise of this Beatitude is staggering: the pure in heart see God. What does this mean? The Jews knew they could not see God with their physical eyes. To even think they could was the heart of idolatry. Yet the Hebrew poets said that we could "see" God in our experience of His love, in our intimate relationship with God (Psalms 17:15; 27:8; 43:2). The Scriptures teach us that we may "gaze" on God's beauty in this world and in the next.

† Seeing God on earth. The pure of heart can see God everywhere. In the writings of spiritual teachers one often reads of seeing God in nature, in the faces of the needy, in the events of human history. Faith and love actually open up our capacity to see the Lord as the reality behind the experiences of our lives. Then we know God is always working in the world; redeeming, caring, and healing. If we become sensitized to God, we learn that He is fully present with us all of the time. To "see" God is to be aware that He is with us and that our lives are hidden with Christ in God.

Religious places have always had a very special meaning to people who love the Lord. It is not that God is more available in churches and shrines; rather, it is that through seeing religious objects and participating in liturgical acts we become keenly aware that God is always present. A woman I know told me she has a special room in her house set aside for meditation and prayer. She said she has a feeling of peace whenever she enters that room, even before she begins her prayers. She has learned what every educator knows, that special environments are important for learning. This Christian woman is better prepared to meet the demands of her life because she has first sought God in the morning. Because of her place of prayer, she has been able to cope in a Christian way with some very difficult problems.

God comes to us in many ways, especially when we read the Bible, and particularly the Gospels. The Holy Spirit inspires our hearts to recognize the Lord in Scripture texts. When we pray the Spirit teaches us something of the reality of the Lord's presence. We see the goodness of the Lord in the testimony of people whose lives have been changed by Him. And we see Him during times of worship, particularly during the Lord's Supper when He comes to us as bread and wine. We see Him imploring us in the eyes of the destitute. The Lord is present in so many forms to those whose eyes are open, who are seeking purity of heart.

† Seeing God in heaven. John the Revelator said that the throne of God and of the Lamb will be visible in the New Jerusalem (the kingdom of glory in heaven). God's servants "will worship Him; they will see Him face to face, and His name will be written on their foreheads. And night will be abolished . . . because the Lord God will be shining on them. They will reign for ever and ever" (Revelation 22:3-5).

The imagery here is profound. The throne (presence) of God is gracious to those who fall down before it. God's name (His essential reality) will be written on their foreheads (showing relationship with God and their witness to Him). Night (death) will be abolished. The light of God (eternal life and blessing) shines on the worshipers.

John's imagery of seeing God face to face represents our knowing and being known by God, as Adam and Eve experienced before the Fall. In heaven God restores our lost innocence and our lost intimacy with Him. John's teaching on seeing God face to face is the fulfillment of hope implied in Paul's statement that in this life we are able to see only "riddles" (1 Corinthians 13:9-13).

In this life we see only reflections of God's glory; in heaven we will see the light of God's perfections. The pure in heart are satisfied with partial sight for the moment because they know the day of full disclosure is ahead. How will we see God in heaven? I do not know the "how," but I believe the seeing will be pure ecstasy for us. God's love in this life is so overwhelming and wonderful! What must it be like in heaven?

Our knowledge of earthly things is really very limited, and our knowledge of divine things even more so. Even our Lord Jesus, who lives in us by His Spirit, is known to us only partially and imperfectly. Until the day when we see Him in all of His resurrected glory, we must be content with the limitations of our "clay pots," as Paul called our bodies. The day is fast approaching when the clay pots will take on an eternal luster and be changed into precious metal.

But though our human sight is limited, our capacity to love is endless. Fullness of love is possible to those who with all their energy seek purity of heart with God and others. For the present, may our love of God and neighbor increase daily until the time when love meets Love in the radiant burst of eternity!

A MEDITATION ON PURITY OF HEART

Who shall go up to the mountain of Yahweh?
Who shall take a stand in His holy place?

The clean of hands and the pure of heart,
whose heart is not set on vanities,
who does not swear an oath in order to deceive.

Such a one will receive blessings from Yahweh,
saving justice from the God of his salvation.

Psalm 24:3-5

OBSERVE A TIME OF SILENCE

BEATITUDE

Blessed are the pure in heart:
they shall see God.

A THOUGHT FOR MEDITATION

"Jesus, the crowning grace impart, Bless me with purity of heart;
That now beholding Thee, I soon may view Thine open face,
On all Thy dazzling beauties gaze, And God for ever see."

Charles Wesley⁴

Lord, give me a pure heart,
so I can love my neighbor as You do.

OBSERVE A TIME OF PRAYER

CLOSING READING

James 1:19-25

NINE

PROCLAIMING PEACE

*B*lessed are the peacemakers: they shall be recognized as children of God.

There is a quaint story from the desert tradition about two monks who lived in the same cell. Their life was very peaceful, but one day, to be like other people, they decided to have a quarrel. What to quarrel about was the question.

One monk said, "I will take this brick, place it between us, and we can quarrel over who owns the brick."

The other monk agreed. It sounded like a good plan. So they sat on the ground facing each other, the brick in the middle.

The first monk said, "This is my brick."

The second monk replied, "No, I believe the brick belongs to me."

Whereupon the first monk retorted briskly, "It is not yours. It is mine!"

The second monk replied, "Very well, if it is really yours, take it!"

Thus ended their attempt at quarreling. The moral of this story is that persons who have forsaken all to follow Christ are not grasping or quarrelsome.

This incident provides us with insight which many Christians in the first four centuries of the church believed crucial for a correct understanding of the Gospel.

† God intends life to have a certain harmonious character about it. To be at peace with others means we are at peace with God and with ourselves.

† Harmonious living is possible for those who really want it. Those monks knew very well how chaotic and violent human nature can be. One of their reasons for going to the desert to live was to escape the atmosphere of hostility they found in the cities. They believed God could change us from violent people to peaceful people, and that our lives could be lived in true love.

† Harmonious living is maintained by a life of self-denial. Only as we become somewhat detached from possessions can we become genuinely peaceful. The peaceful person is in this sense a free person, needing little and wanting nothing.

To those of us who remember World War II, the Korean conflict, Vietnam, and now see international terrorism, the tranquility of these two monks sounds like sheer fantasy. We are so used to violence on television and in the newspapers that we can hardly think of life without it. In spite of all this, the Gospel proclaims peace to those who deny themselves and follow Christ as Lord (Matthew 16:24).

THE SHALOM OF GOD

We must read the historians to sense just how desperate conditions were for the Jews when our Lord spoke to the masses. The first century was a period of rebellion, the roots of which reached back many generations. For the Jews, Roman rule was simply another in a long series of national humiliations at the hands of foreign powers. The Roman shield drove a wedge of hatred between Jew and Gentile. Freedom fighters clustered together in small groups in a vain attempt to liberate the land of Palestine. The Jews were incensed at Roman immorality and polytheism. The savagery of some local Roman officials only added fuel to the fire. To Israel, the emperor was an enemy, perhaps *the* enemy; and the Jews, particularly the young, hungered for a leader who would lead them in covering the fields with Roman blood.

An underlying theme in the Gospels is the confused hope of the people about what Jesus might do in such a situation. His fame as a wonder-worker spread rapidly. People came to Him in droves and rallied around Him with mixed emotions. At times their hopes could not be contained and they tried to make Jesus their king by force. His refusals excited their spirits instead of dampening them. Surely, they thought, He is only waiting for the right moment and then He will act! Even the disciples believed Jesus was the Messiah of the Royal Psalms, the new David who would descend on Israel's enemies with divine fury.

From the perspective of the Jews, their resistance was justified. The land of Palestine was theirs by divine right, and the presence of the Romans seemed to challenge the will of God. Even though the Jews had fought many times to preserve their national identity, they were essentially a peaceful people. *Shalom* (peace) was their greeting and their blessing, on other Jews and strangers alike. Since the Jews had no expansionist policies, to be left alone to worship God and do His will was all they wanted. They felt this was being denied them.

The Roman Empire was held together by its military strength. We have to go all the way back to classical Greece to find a major power whose cohesiveness was based on something other than the capacity to make war. For Israel the idea of peace was more than not being at war. Peace was a way of life.

For the Jews true peace was the gift of God (Numbers 6:23-27; Psalm 4). Happiness and peace were found in the worship of God. The prophets had foretold a coming day of universal peace (Isaiah 9:5-6; 61:1-2). The Messiah would bring God's peace and the lion would lie down by the lamb; soldiers would become farmers and reshape their swords into plowpoints. But in Jesus' day these hopes seemed far away indeed. The peace of Jerusalem was an uneasy peace of weakness, of being broken by a devastating power.

The peace of Jerusalem was wrapped in the Jewish desire for revenge.

This emotional reaction of the people to past generations of oppression made it impossible for Jesus to get a fair hearing. The nation wanted a conquering hero. It wanted Jesus to produce miracles of victory as He did miracles of healing. Although Jesus' message was exactly what the nation needed to hear, the people could not understand a kingdom brought in by self-sacrifice and patience instead of through the agony of war. At this point the shalom of God was only a memory.

JESUS' GIFT OF PEACE

In this Beatitude Jesus was saying that God is a Redeemer who brings peace, that God's people are to prefer peace to violence, and that true believers are to work diligently for the well-being of people everywhere. Whoever does these things will be recognized as God's children, because they live out what God has done. That is, like God, believers deny themselves in order that the world might experience true peace.

Being a peacemaker flows from a right understanding of oneself, a right relationship with God, and an earnest desire to do good to all people. This kind of spirit can be given only by God. It is granted to those who desire to follow God's will, and are willing to sacrifice themselves for it.

The first four Beatitudes set the stage for peacemaking. But it is also necessary that we love mercy and work to free people from oppressive legalisms in order to pave the way for peace. Then and only then are we prepared to step into the role of active peacemaking.

During His last hours our Lord taught His disciples that peace was to dominate their relations with each other *and with the world*. Jesus said to them, "Peace I bequeath to you, My own peace I give you, a peace which the world cannot give, this is My gift to you. Do not let your hearts be troubled or afraid (John 14:27).

† Jesus certainly knew what trouble was, and yet He had a peaceful spirit. Though many believed in Him, He was often rejected, criticized, and even falsely accused. Some of His critics claimed He was filled with demons. Others complained that He broke religious codes. He was accused by some of His own people of being a traitor to Rome. At the last He was mocked, scorned, shamefully treated, brutalized, and murdered. Yet just before He was to suffer the worst, He spoke openly of peace and gave His disciples a mission of peacemaking.

The Gospels make it clear that God was the source of Jesus' peace. Our Lord, as a human being, trusted His Father to such an extent that His own inner being was rested in quiet and patience. Though often upset at the folly of His people and grieved in prayer for their salvation, our Lord enjoyed the contentment that comes from undaunted confidence in God.

Though in His flesh He momentarily drew back from the horrors of the cross, and though He prayed with such intensity that blood oozed from His pores, He resigned Himself to death. Even in His terrible suffering, our Lord was able to endure because He could see beyond it all to the joy that was ahead of Him (Hebrews 12:2). Jesus' inner stability provided Him with divine encouragement and determination. His rest in God was complete, and all the trials and pain He faced on our behalf could not take that away from Him.

† True peace is the gift of Jesus. Jesus' disciples were restless and afraid. I am sure their fears would have ruined them, had they not been given the peace of the Lord. The Gospels show that the disciples did not understand Christ's gift of peace until after the Spirit came at Pentecost. Later, the Apostle Paul wrote of this peace for your benefit and mine.

The fruit of the Spirit is love, joy, peace, patience, kindness, goodness, trustfulness, gentleness and self-

> control; no law can touch such things as these. All
> who belong to Christ Jesus have crucified self with all
> its passions and desires (Galatians 5:22-24).

Notice the cluster of fruit with which peace is identified—virtues evident in the life of our Lord. When it came time for Him to die, He passed these blessings on to the early church, and He gives them to us today if we will receive them. The peace of Jesus is the Spirit of reconciliation He wanted to bring to the world (Romans 5:1-5; Colossians 1:20). It is total reconciliation Jesus offers us—complete reconciliation to God and the possibility of universal reconciliation with each other. Jesus gives us peace and we are to pass His peace to the world.

† Jesus' followers have a ministry of peacemaking. Jesus told the seventy witnesses to say to each house they visited with the Gospel, "Peace to this house" (Luke 10:1-16). This common Hebraic greeting meant much more than just hello. It expressed the desire of the witnesses' hearts that the peace of Christ would fill the lives of everyone in the family. If the household was receptive, peace would remain in it. If the household was not receptive, then peace would be denied. We have come to know that only in Jesus is true and lasting peace possible (John 16:33). And it is only as people come to know Him that our world has any long-range hope of peace. Remember, it was Jesus Himself who told us that worldly attempts to create true peace would fall flat (John 14:27).

With this teaching in mind, we can see why Paul was so upset over divisions in the Corinthian church (1 Corinthians 1:10-16). Jesus' peace is more than just a beautiful idea; it is a working reality in those who receive it (John 17:22-23; Ephesians 4:1-16). The church must be careful not to deny Jesus at this point. Wherever ministers, church boards, denominational leaders, local church officials, and mature members of local churches harbor resentment, spread damaging rumors, agitate discord, speak disparagingly of other brothers and sisters not of their flock, the cross of our Lord Jesus Christ is despised and the church becomes a mockery of the Good News. The witness of the church to the peace of Christ is based on its own acceptance of peace at the cost of self-sacrifice.

   †   The peace of Jesus is not always received. Jesus said that there would be some who would not recognize "the way to peace" (Luke 19:41-44). For whatever reason, some people refuse to let the peace of Jesus come into their hearts. What makes matters worse is that some of them are hostile to anyone who sincerely tries to live the faith. Notwithstanding, the Lord urges us not to allow the insensitivity of others to rob us of our peace. God graciously sends the Holy Spirit into our hearts to cultivate a gentle and restful spirit, even in times of suffering.

PEACEMAKING AS OUR VOCATION

Had Jesus returned at the end of the first century, we would certainly have been spared many difficult moral decisions. None surface more often than how Christians are to witness to human rights and what position Christians are to take on war. Both of these issues relate to our vocation as peacemakers.

    The church is not of the world, yet the church is in the world. This means that as Christians we must bring the word of peace to the world, insofar as it will hear. In making our statement on peace, we must be clear that Christian faith does not permit us to hate anyone. That some Christians do hate brings up the subject of sin and judgment. Christ's call for us to be a peaceful people is basic to our faith and spirituality. But are we not to hate evil as a principle? Yes, but that is tricky. We are not to judge others (Matthew 7:1-5), not to return evil for evil (Romans 12:17), and to leave matters of vengeance to God (Hebrews 10:30). We must follow the implications of our call if we are to be examples of the peacemakers.

    After I had given an address to a men's breakfast group on

peacemaking, a young man approached me with a serious question. He was to register that week, having reached his eighteenth birthday. He was moved by what I had said from Matthew 5:43-48 on loving our enemies and was wondering what to do about registering.

As I looked at the young man, I knew that if he ever entered military service he would be trained to obey orders without regard for his faith, that he would learn how to kill without mercy, and that he might participate in indiscriminate killing, which can hardly be avoided in modern warfare.¹ I knew too if he resisted registration he would be branded a traitor and a coward by those who would not understand his faith, and even by some who would.

While it was not my place to tell him what to do, I did remind him that Jesus said we must treat our enemies with kindness. As we have already seen in the Beatitudes, followers of Christ are expected to be merciful to others. Our Christian faith is one of reconciliation, not strife. On the surface it would seem that anyone taking this kind of position would be applauded. But the fear of our enemies is so great that often we would rather kill them than try to win them through love.

THE VIOLENCE OF JESUS

At times when I am alone I wonder how much of a Christian I really am on this issue of peacemaking. I continually find "good reasons" for justifying my aggressive behavior rather than following Jesus' teaching at face value. That I am not alone in this gives me no comfort. Why is it that our hearts are drawn to the Gospel but our reason pulls us back? I think it is because we are so desperate to protect the illusion that we can control the world; we believe that power is more dependable than love, and that our enemy is beyond appeals to the heart. I also suspect many of us give in too quickly to the self-serving opinions of national interest.

Carlo Carretto is an unusual man. Highly educated and

once holding a prominent salaried position in his church, Carretto heard God's call, left everything, and went to the Sahara Desert to witness to Christ as a member of the Little Brothers Community. Now he is old and writes books, and what he writes troubles me. For example, take the following excerpt from a chapter he wrote dealing with social revolution and the church.

> It is true that Christ is a revolutionary;
> it is true that He is violent,
> but not against others,
> only against Himself.
>
> It is too easy to kill others;
> it is so difficult to die to oneself.
>
> The violence of Christ is the cross;
> it is planted in His heart,
> not in the hearts of His adversaries.
>
> The violence of Jesus is deep love,
> not the sword or the prison,
> which is how we always want to resolve
> the problems which seem insoluble to us.[2]

The violence of Jesus is His cross! The revolution of Jesus is His deep love. Carretto is right. All attempts to justify violent behavior—because Jesus cleansed the temple or castigated some Pharisees or permitted His disciples to have a sword or two between them—are patently ridiculous, when seen in the light of Jesus' trial and crucifixion.

Tournier talks about the chain reaction to violence.[3] One violent act, however small, requires a higher degree of retaliation. This give-and-take gains momentum and intensity until insult becomes war. Even Christians sometimes get caught up in this chain reaction, which is continually fed by our determination to "have our rights." Jesus broke that chain reaction, "by taking upon Himself the violence of men and then refusing . . . to pay back violence for violence."⁴ Jesus absorbed the shocks in order to redeem by self-sacrifice what could not be redeemed by self-defense. It is only when our "selves" are hidden with Christ in God that we are enabled to love like that.

This is what makes Christians supremely happy, even when the world seems to be collapsing around them. They are not happy because things are bad, but because God has revealed Himself to them. God has made them His children! God reveals Himself to children, that is, to those who in simple faith turn to Him as their Father (Luke 10:22). Those who try to live by worldly power alone cannot understand this, just as those who have "seen" the Lord do not themselves covet worldly power. The children of God appear weak, precisely because they are children. However, they are the innocent children who celebrate the reality of an inner peace which they want for the whole world. I believe our childlike prayers will not be in vain.

A MEDITATION ON PEACEMAKING

To Yahweh when I am in trouble
I call and He answers me.

Too long I have lived
among people who hate peace.
When I speak of peace
they are all for war!

Psalm 120:1, 6-7

OBSERVE A TIME OF SILENCE

BEATITUDE

Blessed are the peacemakers:
they shall be recognized as children of God.

A THOUGHT FOR MEDITATION

Hallowed be Thy name, *not mine,*
Thy kingdom come, *not mine,*
Thy will be done, *not mine,*
Give us peace with Thee
Peace with men
Peace with ourselves,
And free us from all fear.

Dag Hammarskjöld[5]

OBSERVE A TIME OF PRAYER

CLOSING READING

1 Corinthians 13:4-7

T E N

ENDURING TRIAL

*B*lessed are those who are
persecuted in the cause of
uprightness:
the kingdom of heaven is theirs.

Like it or not, we all have enemies. I have often heard it said of someone who has recently died, "He didn't have an enemy in the world." That sounds nice and might well be true in the person's hometown. But even the most loving, giving person you know has enemies somewhere. This is also true for you. There are people who hate you not because they know you but because of your skin color, your political party, your nationality, or your social status. Even if these enemies knew you and perhaps admired you personally, they would still hate you and think the earth better off if you were completely out of the way. One thing is certain, painful as it may be: we all have enemies!

Naturally it is easier to live with our enemies if they are far from us. It is quite another thing if they live in the same town, in the same neighborhood. It is worse if they come to us as conquerors and we find ourselves under their power. This was the situation of the Jews in the first century, and of the early church as well. It was partly to prepare His followers for the inevitability of suffering that Jesus pronounced a blessing on those who endured for the kingdom's sake.

THE PEOPLE OF THE WORLD

In the Sermon on the Mount our Lord mentions three groups of people in the world. First there are those who hear the Lord's Word and become His followers. These people are looking for God and recognize that Jesus teaches the truth about God. They, like the disciples (and you and me), attempt to live out the meaning of the Beatitudes. Jesus says these people can be compared with the Old Testament prophets who followed God's will regardless of the cost (Matthew 5:12).

The second group is certainly the largest. It is made up of those whose faith is shallow, who have various kinds of prejudice, and who are headstrong at times. Some of these people do not interpret the sacred writings correctly (5:19), are self-righteous (6:1-7, 16-18), and are judgmental (7:1-5). This second group is pretty set in its ways and probably depends too much on emotion and/or tradition. Their religion is conventional and self-serving.

The third group are those who are hostile to the Gospel, either secretly or openly. They hinder the influence of Jesus' teaching at every turn if they can. They are categorized by our Lord as accusers (5:11-12), enemies (5:43-48), those who are bold in their sins (7:6), and false teachers (7:15-20). These people attack the followers of Christ whenever possible. And because they despise Jesus' teachings on love and justice, they become the special targets of Christian love and concern.

When the Apostle Peter addressed the household of Cornelius, he said that the Lord Jesus was anointed by God and that He went around "doing good and curing all who had fallen into the power of the devil" (Acts 10:38). While the evident goodness of Jesus caused some to praise God, it caused others to become hardened in their hearts—so hard that they eventually killed Him.

It is always a shock to see good people suffer misunderstanding and pain. However, our Lord told us that He came to bring a sword on the earth, not peace (Matthew 10:34-36). But this sword of the Lord was not a blade of steel, but the Word of God, a sword of truth, a coming to grips with reality, bowing before the great God of the universe in repentance and submission. While Jesus did not seek conflict, His message was biting, causing repentance or resistance.

We have already studied Jesus' teaching that Christians are to treat hostile non-Christians with kindness. We are not to retaliate in kind. The Apostle Paul enlarged on this in Romans 12. We are to

> consider others as better and more deserving of grace than ourselves,
> be sure our motives are controlled by goodness,
> do good to those who do evil to us,
> identify with the pain or happiness of others,
> always be humble about our faith,
> be at peace with everyone,
> meet the needs of our enemies whenever we can.

In Romans 13 we read that we are to be respectful of those in positions of power and to love one another.

A persecuted Christian is to be a merciful person, one who counts it all joy to bind up the wounds of the oppressor. The merciful look for good qualities in their oppressors, because all people are made in the image of God and all have sinned. The merciful will not return evil for evil, but good for evil. Indeed, the merciful want to forgive those who treat them badly.

The persecuted Christian is also to be pure in heart, desiring a relationship of innocence and trust with his tormentor. The pure in heart refuses to condemn the persecutor, recognizing that such a person is really tormented by the forces of evil. The tormentor is a victim, just like the ones he persecutes. The pure in heart prays for the persecutor, that his sins will not be held against him. The pure in heart will not allow himself to be dominated by desires for revenge, even though he might legitimately appeal for justice.

The person persecuted for Christ's sake is a peacemaker. He finds strife odious and therefore actively seeks to resolve conflict. He knows that the power of God's love can bring harmony out of chaos. The peacemaker knows that all people are related through creation and may become family members with one another through the grace of God. The peacemaker is overjoyed when hostilities cease.

This is the sword Jesus gives us. The kingdom of heaven belongs to the persecuted because they imitate the love of their Heavenly Father (Matthew 5:48). Such people are deeply joyful because they know that however demeaned they are in the sight of the world, they stand approved by God. The persecuted are so like Christ that they would be delighted to see their tormentors in heaven.

THE HARD REALITIES OF FAITHFULNESS

Being a genuine Christian is at times a frightful thing. Not only do we have to contend with our own sins but also with the sinful acts of those who despise us. It is only by the sustaining grace of God that we are able to overcome.

Jesus repeated this last Beatitude so we would grasp more fully the response we can expect from a suspicious, unbelieving world:

> Blessed are you when people abuse you and persecute you and speak all kinds of calumny against you falsely on My account. Rejoice and be glad, for your reward will be great in heaven; this is how they persecuted the prophets before you (Matthew 5:11-12).

At times, the church has not deserved to be respected and

trusted. Christians have brought shame on Christ by taking aggressive military action against their enemies, by living hypocritical, grasping lives. Some leaders have used the sacrificial gifts of the faithful to live in ease. There have been too many times when the church usurped power for its own benefit. It is only by recapturing a Beatitude spirit that the church can rise above suspicion.

Jesus said that the true church, the church of the Beatitudes spirit, stands in the same honored line of inspiration as the Old Testament prophets. It is a wonderful thing to be named with those faithful people. However, Jesus' teaching connects us with the fate of the prophets as well. It is part of our destiny to be subject to misunderstanding and persecution. What else could we expect from the blindness of unbelief? When our Lord spoke on the mountainside, the kingdom was just dawning. The truths He brought were disturbing and unsettling. "The servant," He said, "is not above his master."

As the Lord's brothers and sisters we are called to die: to renounce self-interest, take up the cross, and follow the Lord. The Lord's instructions to His disciples become our own:

> Be prepared for people to hand you over to Sanhedrins [governments] and scourge you in their synagogues [public places]. . . . But when you are handed over, do not worry about how to speak or what to say . . . the Spirit of your Father will be speaking in you. . . . You will be universally hated on account of My name. . . . If they have called the master of the house "Beelzebul," how much more the members of his household? Matthew 10:17-25

Many years ago Christian missionaries were being recalled from Congo because of severe anti-American feelings there. People were being killed by angry factions, and many of the dead were Christian missionaries. During that time I was having dinner with a leader of one of the mission groups in Congo and asked him if his group was pulling their people out.

"No," he said, without looking up from his plate. "They have been there for years living for Christ. Perhaps this is their time to die for Christ."

This man was not being cavalier about the troubles his missionaries were facing. He simply realized a deep truth: sometimes the only way we can demonstrate the love of God is by taking great personal risks. It was important that young churches not be abandoned during this time of tension. It was more important for the national churches to be loved than for the missionaries to be safe. That conversation has remained vivid in my memory for many years. I cannot help but think of the cross of Christ and of His sacrifical love.

Not only do we stand in the line of the Prophets, but also in the line of the Apostles. The Book of Acts summarizes the persecution they faced by saying the Apostles considered it an honor to suffer humiliation for the sake of Christ's name (Acts 5:40-42).

Persecution is a temporary reaction of an unbelieving world to the Light of Christ. Like a wounded animal lashing out against those who would help, so our enemies lash out against us. Not realizing the real enemy is in their own hearts, they vent their anger and frustration against the church. Such people are to be pitied. Actually, as God would have it, their wrath has served to further the Gospel. Stiff persecution has tended to swell rather than diminish the ranks of the abused church. Besides, those who suffer for Christ are given a special grace to bear up (Revelation 20:4-6). May God enable us to patiently endure whatever distress we must suffer for the cause of our Lord.

ABANDONMENT TO GOD

Our Lord gives us a supernatural joy when we stand firm under unjust treatment; when we bear without malice the hatred directed at us by others; when we are able to be encouraged by brutal treatment rather than cave in; when we turn our attention toward heaven, to God and the benefits of the kingdom.

Perhaps you realize that we have now come full circle in our study of the Beatitudes. The reward of this beatitude is exactly the same as for the first: God's kingdom belongs to the faithful. The humility we read of in the first Beatitude shows itself at its very best in this last Beatitude. The first Beatitude tells us of the struggle we have with our sins before God. This last Beatitude tells us of the struggle we have with our witness before the world. The Beatitudes sandwiched between these two illustrate the depth of submission required by the first and last Beatitudes. All of the joys and blessings which attend Beatitudes two through seven find meaning in the common reward of the first and the last; God's kingdom belongs to the blessed of the Beatitudes.

The progression of thought we see in the Beatitudes calls attention to our need to learn how to live every day in absolute trust in God's good providence. This is not always easy to do because God's presence and intention to bless are not always obvious to us. In his spiritual classic, *Abandonment to Divine Providence*, eighteenth-century writer Jean-Pierre de Caussade helps us cope with the various trials we must endure. You see, Caussade is convinced that all of our life is sacramental because it is graced by God. He also believes that God is literally in control of events and that God's love has our best interests always in mind. When I read Caussade, I come away with three distinct impressions.

Christians need to be completely abandoned to God.

Christians need to keep in mind that things are not always as they appear.

Holiness of heart is gained by performing the duties required of us at the present moment.

These teachings can be very important for us when we suffer misunderstanding or some form of persecution. Let us look briefly at each of them.

† First, we need to learn what it means to be totally abandoned to God. We have encountered this lesson time and again during our study of the Beatitudes. The depth of abandonment Caussade talks about is reached over a period of time. As we grow in the Lord, we see more and more clearly what it means to be totally submitted to His will, trusting Him alone.

> All we must do is submit to everything and be ready for every possibility. In this free offering of the soul to God He demands three things: renunciation, obedience, and love. Everything else is His affair. If we carefully follow the duties imposed on us by our state of life, if we quietly follow any impulse coming from God, if we peacefully submit to the influence of grace, we are making an act of total abandonment.[1]

† Second, as trusting believers we realize that life is not always what it seems to be. This is especially true of pain and trials, for there is no question that Christians suffer. Caussade wants us to know that in our darkest hours, when God seems to be hidden and we are afraid, we can take refuge in the truth that God knows our situation and is going through it with us. Misfortune, illness, spiritual weakness, and persecution are not what they appear to be. Painful? Certainly! But underneath, beyond normal feelings, are the everlasting arms of God.

The Father can keep our hearts at peace in spite of the shattering trials we face. He can penetrate our problems and redeem them through patience and love.

† Third, a holy life and a pure heart are gained as we perform the normal duties of everyday life. We do not need to look for a special calling or location or discipline. Neither do we need extraordinary spiritual gifts or unusual wisdom. If we really want to be

filled with God, all we need do is "fulfill faithfully the simple duties of Christianity and those called for by [our] state of life, accept cheerfully all the troubles [we] meet, and submit to God's will in all [we] have to do or suffer—without, in any way, seeking out trouble for [ourselves]."[2]

This life of abandonment Caussade describes has the Lord Jesus Christ for its center. The ability to live each moment gracefully comes as a gift from God. It is really rather simple: Jesus loves us and we love Him. Because we are inwardly convinced that God is in control, we do not allow worries to control us. Of course, we try to be responsible and caring, for love naturally responds that way. But we do not have to be burdened down with care.

My heart tells me to listen to Caussade. Too often I load up my life with heavy requirements and expectations. Then I do not experience the freedom of faith and rather groan instead of rejoice. If this happens when the going is easy, what will I do when the going is rough? Lord, help me see the Light!

A PATH OF LIGHT IN THE DARK

Psychologist Benedict Groschel observes, "The most significant, persistent, and troublesome challenge to Christian spirituality has always come from the problem of evil."[3] Like moths attracted to flame, we may get too close to evil which, however attractively it is packaged, always means death in the end. Consequently, we can spend a great deal of time in our spiritual development dealing with our sins and trying to keep ourselves from giving in to temptation. In my early Christian life I read a book on temptation which really helped me. The author said that when we Christians sin, we should "fall up," not down. What he meant was that God is always there if we stumble, so we should fall up, into God's arms. That is good advice. We can rest in our Father's arms until the storm is past.

Christian faith is like walking a path of light in the dark. We are bound to meet up with various forms of evil, some of them within our own hearts! Evil breeds chaos and doubt, often forcing us to make decisions we would rather not have to make. But God knows! That is our comfort. In the early stages of spiritual life, we may think that the path will always be beautiful. But life has rough edges for all of us. Actually, we must be tested if our faith is to develop. It will help to remember Caussade's teaching, and also that the treasure of God is contained in "pots of earthenware" (2 Corinthians 4:7-10).

Francis of Assisi believed that the power of love is greater than the power of evil. That hope was put to the test many times. In analyzing Francis' reactions to the stresses produced by evil, Murray Bodo has reached a conclusion that can be of help to us.

> Everything, even evil, is transformed into good by the embrace of divine love; and we do not see things as they are until we take the bold step of overcoming our conventional perceptions of what is attractive and what repulsive by reaching out in love to what is repelling us. [4]
>
> "I say this to you," says our Lord, "love your enemies."

† A MEDITATION ON ENDURANCE

My dear friends, do not be taken aback at the testing by fire which is taking place among you, as though something strange were happening to you; but in so far as you share in the sufferings of Christ, be glad, so that you may enjoy a much greater gladness when His glory is revealed. If you are insulted for bearing Christ's name, blessed are you, for on you rests the Spirit of God, the Spirit of glory.

1 Peter 4:12-14

OBSERVE A TIME OF SILENCE

BEATITUDE

Blessed are those
who are persecuted in the cause of uprightness:
the kingdom of heaven is theirs.

A THOUGHT FOR MEDITATION

"The enemies of Jesus took away everything He had. Naked, He hung on a cross. His foes stood around it, rejoicing. But at the last minute He spoiled their joy by saying, "Father, into Thy hands I surrender My spirit." He had one thing which they could not take from Him. And by this He lives and rules for ever more."   Richard Wurmbrand[5]

OBSERVE A TIME OF PRAYER

CLOSING READING

Revelation 22:13-14

ELEVEN

MEETING HUMAN NEEDS

"*M*aster, which is the greatest commandment of the Law?"

Jesus said to him, "You must love the Lord your God with all your heart, with all your soul, and with all your mind. This is the greatest and first commandment.

The second resembles it: You must love your neighbor as yourself. On these two commandments hang the whole Law, and the Prophets too."

Matthew 22:35-40

The Book of Genesis tells of a time when the inhabited world was quite small and all of its peoples "spoke the same language, with the same vocabulary" (Genesis 11:1). The writer of Genesis does not tell us why, but the unity of the peoples resulted in a challenge to the authority of God. To thwart their efforts to build a tower that would reach the heavens, the abode of God, the Lord confused their language and scattered the peoples over the face of the earth. Thus nationalistic fear was born and from that fear came suspicion, competition, and the need to make war. It is the same today as it was in the distant past!

The Hebrews eventually came to believe that God wanted to restore the unity of the nations and heal their brokenness, that He wanted to create an environment of mutual respect and trust. This would be accomplished when the people came to God in repentance and faith. Israel became the voice of God, appealing to the nations to discover their lost unity and peace through submission to Yahweh, the God of Israel. It never happened, of course, but it is fascinating to think what might have occurred in human history had they done so—or what might happen today if the nations would hear and obey.

This same hope of restoration is basic to the message of the New Testament: the desire for the real unity of the world under the Saviourhood of Jesus Christ, the incarnation of God. In His High Priestly Prayer, our Lord says the world will recognize the validity of His word as the will of God when the disciples are "perfected in unity" (John 17:21-23). The startling thing to me is that the divided, hostile nations would be impressed by the unity of Jesus' followers. At Pentecost the common language of the descending Spirit was in effect the reversal of the confusion of tongues at Babel (Acts 2). It was clear to all in the Upper Room that Jesus is the hope of the world; He provides its peace, its sense of purpose, and its destiny.

But the world still lives in fear, a fear that is compounded because the church is divided against itself. Competition, not compassion, controls relationships between peoples—whether we speak of nations or family members. The church, like Israel, was to have been a sign to the world of the arrival of God's new day. God was bringing a new people into existence, a people for whom friendship and nurture would be more important than power and hostility. Our aggressive nature was to be redirected into projects for the common good. The Lord of life was to be understood as a Servant-leader rather than a Conqueror-controller. One can only wonder what kind of world we would have today had the church been faithful to its peculiar calling.

Given the lethargy that sweeps the Church, it is no longer surprising to me that many Christians can applaud the teachings of Jesus without living them. Many of us have not been sufficiently jarred by the Beatitudes style of commitment to change our lives. We are more comfortable with the status quo, even when we do not particularly like it, than with allowing the Spirit to shake the foundations of our lives. This situation is so widespread and deeply entrenched in the church that one despairs of seeing any significant change. Coupled with this despair is the sense that we Christians have lost something wonderful.

The last four Beatitudes of our Lord attempt to turn us from the fear of people to the love of people, from manipulation to service, from anger to peacemaking, from striking back to submission. The citizens of the kingdom Jesus talks about have a vocation to demonstrate an incredibly unself-seeking love for the rest of the human community. The lifestyle of the Lord is so dramatic that it can only be accomplished in us through the energy of God's grace. The people of God are always miracles of God!

THE LAST FOUR BEATITUDES: A PARAPHRASE

Deeply happy are those whose mercy
knows no bounds:
God will give them unbounded mercy as well!

And joyous are those whose concern
is unobstructed:
they will actually see God's glory!

Inwardly content are those who attempt
to resolve conflicts:
They are the children of God!

Truly fulfilled are those who suffer rejection

and pain because they follow God's way:
God's kingdom belongs to them!

The common theme of the last four Beatitudes is that *selfless love for the benefit of one's neighbor is blessed by God*. By neighbor, as we have seen, Jesus means anyone who is in need of help, whether friend or foe. Even though this is the general standard for God's new people, our Lord suggests differing ways of approaching others. In the Sermon on the Mount we see that the faithful are to be accepted immediately, openly and with joy, just as we would accept the Lord Jesus Himself; those who are hostile we accept with caution. What we do with a Christian who breaks covenant with the Lord and fellowship with the church is another matter, beyond the scope of this book (1 Corinthians 5:9-13; Jude 20-23). The point is that we are to always freely love those who have needs, and meet those needs to the best of our ability. Sometimes that kind of love is tough; sometimes it is tender. But it always has the best interests of the other person in mind.

In our summary of the first four Beatitudes in Chapter 6, we noticed that the first three were generally concerned with self-emptying and the fourth with being filled (with God). There is a similar pattern in the last four Beatitudes. Beatitudes five through seven are concerned with giving, while eight is one of receiving. But recall the stark contrast. In the fourth Beatitude, the believer receives the fullness of God's presence. In the eighth Beatitude the believer receives the hostility of the world. In the first four Beatitudes the believer receives something (grace) for nothing (spiritual poverty). In the eighth Beatitude the believer receives nothing (hostility, absence of love) for something (good works as seen in Beatitudes five through seven).

LOVING OUR NEIGHBOR

To love our neighbor means to attempt to meet the needs of that person in some way. Our service ranges from ardent prayers on that person's behalf to acts of self-denial, in some extreme instances it can mean death. As we think about the last four Beatitudes we take note of some special concerns.

† Beatitude five: The special focus of mercy is toward those who have the least, specifically the poor, the disadvantaged, even the undeserving. These are people who can only receive but cannot return our gift of love. As such, they are constant reminders of the first Beatitude which says the kingdom is given only to those who recognize they are spiritually bankrupt.

† Beatitude six: If we are truly Christ's followers we will look past outward appearances to people's hearts. It is crucial never to judge quickly, since outward appearances can be deceiving. We should be especially able to accept other Christians openly and warmly, with no strings attached. Undue suspicion should be avoided at any cost. The pure in heart, those who relate to others with an innocent attitude, do not lay heavy spiritual obligations on others. Instead we are to model love and care for people, always doing our best to secure their freedom in Christ.

† Beatitude seven: As Jesus' followers we know that anger and hostile reactions demean other people. We know that we were created to live in harmony with others, with ourselves, and with nature. Therefore Christians turn from violence and instead look for any possibility of reconciliation. In fact, we are willing to absorb violence, if necessary, in an attempt to stop it. The compassion of Jesus also leads us to work hard for human rights.

It is natural for Christians to do works of mercy in a spirit of innocence and charity. It is important for us to do these works in such a way that it is obvious they are done in the name of the Lord Jesus. We recognize this will be offensive to some people and may even become a barrier between us. While this is not what we want, at times the Christian message of God's love is confrontive, especially when Jesus disturbs the conscience. Unfortunately this will occasionally mean some form of persecution for us. When this happens we will simply have to trust the grace of God so that we can bear our pain with fortitude and love.

† Beatitude eight: To be persecuted is to have something demeaning or physically harmful done to us. Jesus gives us some straight talk abut the nature of this persecution, when He says we might be abused, talked about in an evil way, and harassed (Matthew 5:12). He states further that this happens because the world "hates" and "persecutes" us because of that hatred (John 15:18-20). Also, the Lord says the "enemy" will "judge" us and "beat" us, even putting some of us to "death" (Matthew 10:17ff). Returning evil for good shows how warped the perspective of the world is.

The last four Beatitudes comprise what Jesus means by loving one's neighbor as oneself. For us love is a two-sided coin with God on one side and our neighbor on the other. Christianity is a combination of vital faith and loving-kindness. Of course, in terms of grace, love of God precedes love of neighbor.

THE PROMISES OF BLESSING

† Christ says the merciful will receive mercy from God, and perhaps from some people as well. This Beatitude demonstrates the so-called Golden Rule, doing to others what we would like done to ourselves under similar circumstances. However, we do not give mercy to change others but because they need mercy. We have deep feelings toward people because we have received mercy from God.

It needs to be repeated that our good works do not gain us favor with God. We have been reconciled to God by grace through faith. Good works, however sacrificial, cannot gain us an entrance into the kingdom. We should thank God for this central biblical truth. Just think how confused and paranoid we would become if we tried to figure out how many good works it would take to satisfy the Lord. This would pull us into a vicious, self-defeating cycle of introspection. Christ has made us free! Let us love freely in return!

† The pure in heart "see" God. This is true when we see Jesus

in those who suffer hardships (the sick, the prisoners, the naked, the hungry). We also see God everywhere because saving faith has made life transparent. There is a sense in which we see God everywhere because we know God is Creator and Sustainer of the world. But the best is yet to come! We will see God in His glory in the heavens. We will see the light that is God and feel the warmth that is God's love, and that will be heaven indeed. What greater blessing can we know than this?

† The peacemakers are recognized by their deeds as members of God's family. Who recognizes them as such? Certainly the church, that is, other believers, and perhaps even some nonbelievers. But Jesus seems to be saying here that God recognizes peacemakers as His children. Peacemakers bear their Father's likeness: *unself-conscious love*. Like their common Lord, peacemakers sacrifice themselves to see peace abound. This is their vocation, notwithstanding their own inner struggles and the overwhelming presence of evil in the world.

However, evil bears witness against itself, by its manifestation in pain, misery, brokenness, and death. Deliberate evil has a self-consuming character. It ravages what it can and then turns on itself. In one sense, the evil which people find in themselves is their own worst enemy. Peacemakers are the archrivals of evil, especially in announcing the forgiveness of sins through Jesus Christ.

† The persecuted are able to endure hostility because the Spirit in them witnesses that true peace comes only through repentance, confession, and turning from the illusions of sin. Such persons experience the kingdom of God as a divine gift! For that reason the Beatitudes end with the same promise with which they began: *the kingdom of God belongs to the Beatitudes people*. Like the poor in spirit, the persecuted are powerless unless the Lord comes to help them. Sometimes the Lord is pleased to deliver them from their immediate problems. Other times, for reasons hidden in the divine wisdom, believers must suffer, perhaps even become martyrs. Delivered or not, the kingdom is waiting for those

who have suffered for Jesus' sake.

Indeed, the kingdom is waiting for everyone who is really poor in spirit. This is the message of the first Beatitude and it colors all the rest of them. Because this is true, Christians who have been privileged to live their lives in relative peace can behold the kingdom as much as any martyr ever has. Their humility, born of confessed sin and dependence on God, admits them into the kingdom of glory. While we live, however, we must keep our faith alive for we never know when we may be called on to witness with our blood.

A life of such mercy, purity, peace, and endurance is blessed by God the Father, and fills us with heavenly graces that come from the Holy Spirit. The Beatitudes move us in the direction of becoming more like God. Such a life is genuinely happy and fulfilling.

THE CHURCH HELPS US GROW

We do not live the Christian life alone. Not only do we have the constant help and inspiration of the Holy Spirit, but we have one another in the church. The church is the gathering of the "called," those who have heard the voice of the Lord in their hearts, calling them to seek Christ and live. In the church's worship, its life of collective prayer, the reception of the Holy Communion, through festive celebrations, and in its preaching and teaching, our spirits are fed with the vision of eternal life. The church as the body of Christ in the world helps us with the tensions of the Beatitudes life by being an accepting, nurturing, risking, boundary-setting community of Jesus.

† The church as an accepting community. The church of Jesus thrives on failures and rejects, people whose world has crumbled, who cannot "get their act together." The church has always been a grass-roots movement, usually among the poorer classes. The fact that God came "down" to identify with us is what

redeems us. The downward mobility of God is also incarnated in the church.—The church is one beggar telling another beggar where to get bread.[1]

The plain fact is that we humans need help from the outside! When the church fulfills its God-given role, it provides an atmosphere of warmth and acceptance. It is tragic that many find the institutional church cold and uncaring. While the visible church needs the life-giving breath of the Spirit to blow fire into it again, the invisible church, the church of those born of God, continues to offer Christ as the living Bread and Light of the world. We may need a few cathedrals to honor the living God, but most of our churches should have the air of a soup kitchen, spooning out food for the hungry, with absolutely no concern for social status.

† The church as a nurturing community. To nurture is to help grow. The Scripture describes spiritual life as the process of growing from infancy to adulthood. One thing this means is that there are no instant saints. There can be no doubt that God sometimes makes vast sweeping changes in our lives, but most of our growth comes through prolonged struggle. Wisdom is gained with time, trial and error, waiting before God in prayer, and saturating oneself with Scripture. Such wisdom is given to those who persevere in faith. Patience is the heartbeat of spiritual growth.

The church is the invisible mother of spiritual life. I say invisible because we do not normally see this reality as we sit in the pew and look around us at those who have come to worship. Everyone there is in the same shape—needing help, desperate for life and purpose. But rising up from individual members of the church, somewhere between stained glass and creed, is the spirit of love and grace. It is a "real presence" of life from which we drink and grow. It may come through one another, through the preached Word, through the sacraments, through order and silence.

The church learns how to give mercy to the world by first giving it to its members—and receiving it from them in return. There is little use in talking about healing a fractured world until we learn how to live at peace with one another. It is as we nurture and are nurtured that we learn what it means to live with unmixed motives. It is through hearing what the Scripture says, not what we want it to say, that we become perfected in love. We must care about the progress each of us makes in the Lord in order that we may fulfill our mission in the world.

† The church as a risking community. Almost everyone is cautious about taking risks. Most of us simply do not have a high-wire mentality. We like the security of the net below. But the church is called to take tremendous risks. Jesus is our example in this, as in every aspect of authentic spirituality. He called as disciples some people with shady reputations. He associated with social rejects such as prostitutes. He attended fashionable dinner parties and was called a glutton and a social drinker. Jesus' actions scandalized the purists. In each case, of course, Jesus was doing the Father's will. His risks were redemptive, but at the same time, they were subject to misunderstanding and scandal. The church is called to bear a witness to Christ in the throes of worldly life, without being victimized by it.

When the church takes seriously being merciful to people, trying to act as a peacemaker, and refraining from treating others legalistically, it becomes a risking community. It risks its credibility, risks becoming a reproach on the neighborhood, risks losing moneyed members, or even being attacked in some instances. But if the church is to be Christ's body, it can do nothing less than lay down its life and die.

† The church as a boundary-setting community. It is the church's responsibility to constantly remind its members what Christian baptism means: death to the world and life in Christ. If baptism means anything, it means a certain lifestyle, a commitment to things pure and good. By boundaries I do not mean an uncaring legalism. We are done with that in Christ. I mean the reaffirmation that we need to make to basic biblical principles of attitude and behavior. This means establishing limits. There are don'ts as well as

do's. But in defining Christian behavior, we must always commit ourselves to love and care for one another.

Boundary-setting cannot become legalistic if we remember three things: any boundary established must conform to the biblical source; boundaries need to be openly discussed periodically in order to see if they continue to apply to the needs of the community; boundaries must be enforced with love and patience.

This is to say that any boundary established by a group of believers must reflect a Beatitudes spirit. Therefore, the following ought to guide us in establishing the parameters of our fellowship.

Beatitude	Attitude
1	Deep humility before God and one another
2	Awareness of one's own sin and sincere prayer for the sins of the church and the world
3	Listening attentively to what pleases God
4	Seeking an upright life before God
5	A sincere desire to show mercy
6	A fear of placing legalistic requirements on brothers and sisters
7	Zeal for keeping the spirit of peace in the church
8	A willingness to accept criticism without becoming defensive

The church is a temporary spiritual formation community preparing its members for works of mercy in the world and entrance into the kingdom on the day of the Lord.

Grant me, most loving Jesus,
Thou best of masters,
that I may, with a holy thirst,
drink from the streams of Thy saving teaching.
May I diligently study, wisely understand,
sweetly taste, peacefully enjoy the sacred words

of Thy mouth, and carefully fashion
all my discipline according to their guidance.

For nowhere do I so readily
and so clearly find the way of perfection
as in the bright mirror of Thy Holy Gospel,
laid open to me and all [people] for our study.[1]

This is a helpful prayer as we apply ourselves to the task of discovering what makes God smile. Our main comfort is that we have the Holy Spirit as our faithful Guide and gentle Teacher. The lessons He teaches are eternal.

✝ A MEDITATION ON LOVE

"Master, which is the greatest commandment of the Law?" Jesus said to him, "You must love the Lord your God with all your heart, with all your soul, and with all your mind. This is the greatest and first commandment. The second resembles it: You must love your neighbor as yourself. On these two commandments hang the whole Law, and the Prophets too."

Matthew 22:35-40

OBSERVE A TIME OF SILENCE

BEATITUDE

Blessed be Yahweh for ever.
Amen. Amen.

Psalm 89:52

A THOUGHT FOR MEDITATION

"To disappear from the world as an object of interest in order to be everywhere in it by hiddenness and compassion is the basic movement of the Christian life."[2]

St. Paul says our lives are "hidden with Christ in God." What does that mean for my relationships with others?

OBSERVE A TIME OF PRAYER

CLOSING READING

Matthew 5:38-48

TWELVE

CRY JOY!

Alleluia!
Praise Yahweh, all nations,
extol Him, all peoples,
for His faithful love is strong
and His constancy never-ending.

—Psalm 117

The Beatitudes are not easy reading. The obligations taught in these simple sayings are overwhelming, calling as they do for a heart totally devoted to the love of God and to service for others. At times, I want to jump on the bandwagon of those commentators who say the Beatitudes describe life in the future kingdom, not in this world. After all, who can live with these teachings as the benchmarks of true faith?

Jesus told His disciples to follow Him. It sounds so easy, "Walk along with Me and learn." Tagging along with the Lord, we suddenly find ourselves leaving the valley of illusion where we have lived so long and feel so at home. We enter a new world which leaves us dangling in the air—groping wildly for anything to hold on to. We are exposed here for what we are, and for all to see. The language we hear is strange; it is the sound of prayer, praise, and singing so loud it stuns us. The sights we see are beyond description, and we are torn between fear and ecstasy. The only decision is whether to run or drop to our knees!

Confession is painful and yet it has become for me a way of life. You see, once you catch a glimpse of the deep joy there is in God and realize—I mean deeply understand—that God is love and that He wants you to share His life, you are forever changed. Then the Beatitudes become believable and desirable. Then you also realize you can no more do without these teachings than you can live without food or air. So confession pours out of your heart like swollen streams from a broken dam, for confession is the gateway to happiness. When God comes into your pain, drawing you close and covering you with His healing love, you reach out to embrace the Father and cry joy!

In the Beatitudes, Jesus teaches of a life that pleases God, made possible by God's grace. Without His enabling power, the Beatitudes must remain only fond hopes. But with His grace, they become the life of the kingdom present as well as of the kingdom future. Make no mistake about it, these teachings of Jesus wrench confession out of us. At the same time, they crown our lives with Gospel happiness as we walk with Jesus toward the Father's house.

A spiritual teacher once said that our vocation as Christians is "to begin on earth the life and liturgy of heaven."¹ The Beatitudes provide the life and it just may be they provide the liturgy too. These sayings of Jesus are a litany of the way of salvation, sung in chorus by the redeemed. Maybe they are also an antiphonal chant, thundered out in the heavens by the "winged creatures." Surely they form a confession of faith for those who have lost themselves in Christ. The Beatitudes seem to have a hymnic quality about them—they read like a responsive reading between Christ and His church. And with what glory they speak of the loving care of God! They have also become a sermon for everyone of us! Prayer—yes, they are prayer as well.

Life and liturgy—those words describe what writing this book has meant to me. It has been both study and poetry, hard work and sheer joy. Life and liturgy. If you read the Sermon on the

Mount, you will discover that Jesus followed the Beatitudes by telling those who heard Him that they were the salt of the earth and the light of the world. Having looked rather closely at these Beatitudes, we can see that anyone who takes them to heart is, in fact, salt and light. But there is a warning as well, about salt turned bad and light hidden away. However, when salt is used and the light shines, then God is glorified. That is happiness indeed!

We have tried to hear the Beatitudes as though we were standing in the weary crowd Jesus spoke to that day. Understanding them better has helped us see how contemporary they are, and how easily they apply to our lives. The Beatitudes are life and liturgy to all who in desperation turn to Him who is both Lord and God. With this in mind, the following paraphrase of these eight love songs from God has emerged.

THE LIFE THAT PLEASES GOD

How deeply happy are those who recognize
their need of God:
God's Kingdom belongs to them!

And joyous are those who are alarmed
because of sin:
God will rescue them from it!

Inwardly content are those who listen
attentively to God:
They will receive as a gift what belongs
to God!

Truly fulfilled are those who really want
to live an upright life:
They will get their heart's desire!

Deeply happy are those whose mercy
knows no bounds:
God will give them unbounded mercy!

And joyous are those whose concern
is unobstructed:
They will actually see God's glory!

Inwardly content are those who attempt
to resolve conflicts:
They are the children of God!

Truly fulfilled are those who suffer pain
and rejection because they follow God's way:
God's kingdom belongs to them!

MAJOR MOTIFS IN THE BEATITUDES

There are five major motifs running through the Beatitudes. The first of these is also the central theme of the Beatitudes.

    †   The primary concern of the Beatitudes is the renunciation of self-will. The short prayer of Jesus in the Garden of Gethsemane reflects this idea of self-denial. Speaking to the Father, Jesus said, "Let Your will be done, not Mine" (Luke 22:43). This attitude is what Christian psychiatrist Gerald May calls "willingness." Jesus bowed willingly to the desires of His Father in heaven, even though such submission was to bring Him pain and anguish. This is a surrender of "self-separateness" from God. That is, it is possible to want to do God's will so much that we do not see our own will as separate from God's will. If God wants something, then that is what we do, immediately and without debate. May calls this an "entering into" God with complete abandon.[2]

        May contrasts willingness with "willfullness" or setting one-self apart from God "in an attempt to master, direct, control, or otherwise manipulate existence."[3] This is the essence of rebellion, pride, defensiveness, greed, and fear. In Psalm 2 the Lord "laughs" at those arrogant enough to attempt to set themselves against God and His anointed. Certainly the Gospel message is the overcoming of willfulness with willingness, with regard to the will of God. This requires a conscious decision to do only the will of God and to accept whatever is necessary to bring that about.

In terms of the idea of willingness, the first four Beatitudes are concerned with the Father and the last four with the neighbor. The ground of this willingness is humility, defined by Paul as making our own "the mind of Christ" (Philippians 2:5-11). Because of His humility, Jesus was rewarded for His willingness to do only the Father's will. In this, He becomes our example.

† The second major motif is that the power which reconciles us to God and each other is divine grace. The Beatitudes speak of a gifted and graced life which is not a product of human ingenuity.

† Third, the forces of evil actively conspire to defeat any attempt by us to submit to the influence of the Beatitudes. Although the "wiles" of the devil are many and varied, we will look at only four of the most common problems we face in developing spiritually.

> We cannot advance far in the spiritual life if we think God is out to get us. In the Beatitudes, God is shown as a loving, supporting, patient God whose good providences work on our behalf. If we are seeking God, we need not fear His wrath.

> We must be careful not to spend our time on secondary matters. If we have trouble recognizing primary issues, we need to consult with our spiritual friends and spend time in reflection and prayer. In any case, our attitude is to be one of love and reconciliation.

> We need to avoid compromising the expectations of the Lord Jesus. Compromise comes from wilfullness and can be overcome only by prayer and renewed abandonment to God.

> One problem we are likely to face is despair. Many Christians begin to question their faith when they go through a dry period. Spiritual guides have recog-

nized this as a trick of the Evil One. God is always with those who seek Him, and faith is able to sense God's presence when our feelings tell us He is gone. Admittedly it is difficult to overcome the idea that spirituality can be identified with our feelings and with obvious answers to prayer. In our prayer periods, remembering that salvation is a gift of grace received through faith will help us keep our balance. Meditation on Paul's description of the armor of God in Ephesians 6:10-20 may also be meaningful.

† Fourth, the selfless love to which God calls you and me produces a deep joy in our hearts. This joy or happiness of the Spirit has three dimensions.

Joy is the assurance of faith that we are acceptable to God and that God's good providences are working on our behalf. This joy is an inner calm produced by confidence in God. It is untouched by outward circumstances and is not diminished by pain and sorrow.

Sometimes this joy gives us a sense of satisfaction and comfort.

The highest level of joy is a kind of ecstasy or overflowing happiness. There is no way of describing this—no more than we can say what it is like to be in love. It is simply a graced moment, and may last only a short time. We are cautioned by spiritual guides not to seek this experience. God gives it when it pleases Him—it is always a by-product of faith.

† Finally, the ultimate goal of Christian spirituality is to behold the glory of God in the kingdom of heaven. It is for this we wait in eager anticipation because we have been taught by the Holy Spirit that this is the destiny of the people of God.

GROWING IN CHRIST

The Beatitudes provide us with many helpful insights on how to grow in Christ. I would like to recall some of the more important ones for our spiritual growth.

† Developing intimacy with God takes time. Sometimes our relationship with God seems more like starts and stops than a flowing sense of God's presence. This is why we need to make conscious commitments of love to God. Expressions of adoration and reaffirmations of love are important to any relationship. Give them freely.

† Honesty is always the best policy in spiritual matters. We need to develop an intimate, transparent relationship with God through prayer and obedience. On the last page of this book I recommend several excellent books on prayer. Just as marriage enrichment seminars can make our marriages better, good books on prayer can open new experiences with the Lord for us.

† We always need the support of a worshiping community of faith. The church is vital to our growth. As we prepare for worship, we can begin to focus our attention on God. Sharing in the Lord's Supper should become especially meaningful. This is more than a memorial service. The Lord is with us in a unique way during the Communion. Knowing exactly how He is present is not the main issue for me; rather, being open to Him in love and obedience is the key.

† In our prayers and meditation we need to ask the Father to help us become more sensitized to the needs of others, especially our families. Remember, in ministering to others we minister to Christ Himself. The Lord shows up in the needs of people. Sometimes we entertain angels without knowing it!

† We need to be aware of how controlled we have been by the values of our culture. I am not condemning social customs and values. I am saying that we need to be free of anything that would weigh us down in our pursuit of spiritual life.

✝   Finally, we need to rest in God's love at all times, but especially when we sin. It is rather easy to get our eyes off of God's love when we are filled with guilt and self-disgust. But God is gracious and if we remember Him, He will come to us with forgiveness and warmth.

A PARTING WORD

Like all interpreters of Scripture, I dread the thought of disappointing God by making either more or less of Jesus' words than He did. But all of us have a bias which is shaped by our experiences. I don't think we can ever fully get away from that influence. However, we can make sincere efforts to follow the Lord as closely as possible. I have tried to do this and I know you are doing the same.

I have another feeling that is difficult to put into words. Perhaps the following one sentence sermon by a spiritual guide might get my point across. With a wry smile on his face he said, "All I do is sit by the bank of the river, selling river water."[4]

The water of life is all around us, free for the taking. The most important thing is our desire to have it. When we want the Lord with all our hearts, He will come with grace and love. Our lives will take on an inexpressible happiness and, with the angels and all the company of heaven, we will go on our way crying joy!

✝

A MEDITATION ON OUR SPIRITUAL JOURNEY

Allelulia!
Praise Yahweh, all nations,
extol him, all peoples,
for His faithful love is strong
and His constancy never-ending.

Psalm 117

OBSERVE A TIME OF SILENCE

BEATITUDE

Blessed be the Lord day after day,
He carries us along, God our Saviour.

Psalm 68:19

A THOUGHT FOR MEDITATION

Christ Himself sometimes describes the Christian way as very hard, sometimes as very easy. He says, 'Take up your cross'—in other words, it is like going to be beaten to death in a concentration camp. Next minute He says, 'My yoke is easy and My burden light.' He means both.

C.S. Lewis[5]

OBSERVE A TIME OF PRAYER

CLOSING READING

Hebrews 12:1-4

SELECTED READINGS IN CHRISTIAN SPIRITUALITY

I have found the following books on prayer to be of special value. They represent both Christian east and west. I suggest you read them in the following order:

> *Beginning to Pray* by Anthony Bloom
> *Letters from the Desert* by Carlo Carretto
> *Centering Prayer* by Basil Pennington
> *The Way of a Pilgrim* edited by Helen Bacovcin
> *The Lover and the Beloved* by John Michael Talbot

For general spiritual reading I suggest the following:

> *The Way of the Heart* by Henri Nouwen
> *The Cost of Discipleship* by Dietrich Bonhoeffer
> *The Imitation of Christ* by Thomas à Kempis (E. M. Blaiklock, translator)
> *New Seeds of Contemplation* by Thomas Merton
> *My All for Him* by Basilea Schlink
> *Abandonment to Divine Providence* by Jean-Pierre de Caussade
> *The Little Flowers of St. Francis* translated by Raphael Brown.

For those who want a special challenge I suggest:

> *Compassion* by Donald P. McNeil, et. al.
> *Way of the Ascetics* by Tito Coliander
> *The Ladder of Divine Ascent* by John Climacus
> *Will and Spirit* by Gerald G. May.

FOR FURTHER READING

The following materials are suggested to help you increase your understanding of Spiritual Formation, and more importantly, to help you grow in your faith. Readings are categorized under basic headings having to do with our formation. Most of the books are in print at the time of this compilation. The few which are not can be obtained from most college and seminary libraries in your area. In addition to these resources, please use the footnotes as a further means of exploring the various topics developed in this book.

General Readings
1. Leslie Weatherhead, *The Transforming Friendship*
2. Steve Harper, *Devotional Life in the Wesleyan Tradition*
3. Maxie Dunnam, *Alive in Christ*
4. E. Stanley Jones, *The Way*
5. Henri Nouwen, *Making All Things New*
6. Evelyn Underhill, *The Spiritual Life*
7. Alan Jones & Rachel Homer, *Living in the Spirit*
8. Iris Cully, *Education for Spiritual Growth*
9. Benedict Groeschel, *Spiritual Passages*

Scripture
1. Robert Mulholland, *Shaped by the Word*
2. David Thompson, *Bible Study That Works*
3. Susan Muto, *A Guide to Spiritual Reading*
4. Thomas Merton, *Opening the Bible*
5. H.A. Nielsen, *The Bible As If for the First Time*

Prayer

1. Harry E. Fosdick, *The Meaning of Prayer*
2. Dick Eastman, *The Hour That Changes the World*
3. Kenneth Leech, *True Prayer*
4. Anthony Bloom, *Beginning to Pray*
5. Maxie Dunnam, *The Workbook of Living Prayer*
6. O. Hallesby, *Prayer*

The Lord's Supper

1. William Willimon, *Sunday Dinner*
2. William Barclay, *The Lord's Supper*
3. Martin Marty, *The Lord's Supper*

Fasting

1. Richard Foster, *Celebration of Discipline* (helpful chapter)
2. Tilden Edwards, *Living Simply Through the Day* (helpful chapter)

Direction/Accountability

1. David Watson, *Accountable Discipleship*
2. Tilden Edwards, *Spiritual Friend*
3. Kenneth Leech, *Soul Friend*
4. Robert Coleman, *The Master Plan of Evangelism*

Personality and Spiritual Development

1. David Keirsey, *Please Understand Me*
2. Harold Grant, *From Image to Likeness*
3. Christopher Bryant, *The River Within*
4. Chester Michael, *Prayer and Temperament*

The Holy Spirit

1. Billy Graham, *The Holy Spirit*
2. Kenneth Kinghorn, *The Gifts of the Spirit*

3. Myron Augsburger, *Quench Not the Spirit*

Discipline and Disciplines
1. Richard Foster, *Celebration of Discipline*
2. Gordon MacDonald, *Ordering Your Private World*
3. Albert E. Day, *Discipline and Discovery**
4. James Earl Massey, *Spiritual Disciplines*
5. Maxie Dunnam, *The Workbook of Spiritual Disciplines*

History of Christian Spirituality
1. Urban Holmes, *A History of Christian Spirituality*
2. Alan Jones & Rachel Hosmer, *Living in the Spirit* (helpful chapter)

Devotional Classics (Introduction to)
1. Tilden Edwards, *The Living Testament: The Essential Writings Since the New Testament*
2. Thomas Kepler, *An Anthology of Devotional Literature*
3. *The Upper Room Devotional Classics*
4. Paulist Press Series, *The Classics of Western Spirituality*

Social Spirituality
1. John Carmody, *Holistic Spirituality*
2. William Stringfellow, *The Politics of Spirituality*
3. Dietrich Bonhoeffer, *Life Together*
4. Thomas Kelly, *A Testament of Devotion* (helpful chapter)
5. Henri Nouwen, *Gracias!*
6. Henri Nouwen, *Compassion*

Ministry and Spiritual Formation
1. Edward Bratcher, *The Walk-on-Water Syndrome*
2. Henri Nouwen, *The Living Reminder*
3. Louis McBirney, *Every Pastor Needs a Pastor*

4. Henri Nouwen, *Creative Ministry*
5. Oswald Sanders, *Spiritual Leadership*

Devotional Guides and Prayer Books

1. Rueben Job, *The Upper Room Guide to Prayer for Ministers and Other Servants*
2. Bob Benson, *Disciplines for the Inner Life*
3. John Baille, *A Diary of Private Prayer*
4. Charles Swindoll, *Growing Strong in the Seasons of Life*
5. John Doberstein, *The Minister's Prayer Book*
6. *The Book of Common Prayer*

NOTES

Chapter One

1. Quoted in Benedict J. Groeschel, *Spiritual Passages: The Psychology of Spiritual Development* (New York: Crossroad, 1984), p. xxi.

2. Unless stated otherwise, all Scripture quoted in this book is from the *New Jerusalem Bible*. It should be noted that Beatitudes numbers two and three are reversed in the *New Jerusalem Bible*. They are retained here in their traditional listing. However, the promise of the gentle inheriting the earth does seem like a natural companion idea to the poor inheriting the kingdom of heaven.

3. Clarence Jordan, *The Cotton Patch Version of Paul's Epistles* (New York: Association Press, 1968), p. 105.

Chapter Two

1. Thomas Merton, *New Seeds of Contemplation* (New York: New Directions, 1961), p. 51.

2. Ecclesiasticus 3:18-21, *New Jerusalem Bible.*

3. Carlo Carretto, *Summoned by Love* (Maryknoll: Orbis Books, 1982), p. 19.

4. Thomas Merton, *No Man Is an Island* (New York: Harcourt Brace Jovanovich, 1955), p. 121.

Chapter Three

1. Regis J. Armstrong and Ignatius C. Brady, *Francis and Clare: The Complete Works* (New York: Paulist Press, 1982), p. 103.

2. *Ibid.*, p. 152.

3. Carlo Carreto, *Letters from the Desert* (Maryknoll: Orbis Books, 1972), p. 21.

Chapter Four

1. Dietrich Bonhoeffer, *The Cost of Discipleship* (New York: The MacMillan Company, 1970), p. 171.

2. *Ibid.*, p. 165.

3. Arnaldo Fortini, *Francis of Assisi* (New York: The Crossroad Company, 1985), p. 500.

4. Albert C. Outler (ed.), *The Works of John Wesley*, vol. I, *The Sermon* (Nashville: Abingdon Press, 1984), vol. I, p. 494.

5. Charles Cummings, *The Mystery of the Ordinary* (New York: Harper and Row, Publishers, 1982).

6. John Climacus, *The Ladder of Divine Ascent* (New York: Paulist Press, 1982), p. 147.

7. Simeon the New Theologian, *The Discourses* (New York: Paulist Press, 1980), p. 331.

8. Andrew Murray, *Humility* (Springdale: Whitaker House, 1982), pp. 47-48.

Chapter Five

1. Benedicta Ward (tr.), *The Sayings of the Desert Fathers* (Kalamazoo: Cistercian Publications, Inc., 1984), p. 183.

2. Thomas Merton, *Thoughts in Solitude* (New York: Farrar, Straus, and Giroux, 1982), p. 83.

3. Henry Scougal, *The Life of God in the Soul of Man* (Philadelphia: The Westminster Press, 1948), pp. 53-55.

4. Thomas à Kempis, *The Imitation of Christ* (Nashville: Thomas Nelson Publishers, 1979), p. 26.

Chapter Six

1. G.E. Palmer, et. al. (tr. & ed.), *The Philokalia* (London: Faber and Faber, 1979), vol. I, p. 194.

2. Carlo Carretto, *Letters from the Desert* (Maryknoll: Orbis Books, 1981), pp. 55-56.

3. Thomas R. Kelly, *A Testament of Devotion* (New York: Harper and Row, Publishers, 1941), p. 92.

4. Dietrich Bonhoeffer, *The Cost of Discipleship* (New York: The Macmillan Company, 1970), p. 181.

Chapter Seven

1. Thomas Merton, *Love and Living* (New York: Farrar, Straus, Giroux, 1979), p. 203.

2. Malcolm Muggeridge, *Something Beautiful for God* (New York: Harper and Row Publishers, 1971), pp. 74-75.

3. Mother Teresa of Calcutta, *Life in the Spirit* (San Francisco: Harper and Row, Publishers, 1983), pp. 37-87.

Chapter Eight

1. Shel Silverstein, *Where the Sidewalk Ends* (New York: Harper and Row, 1974), p. 19.

2. John P. Meier, *Matthew* (Delaware: Mich and Glazier, Inc., 1983), p. 41.

3. Thomas Merton, *No Man Is an Island* (New York: Harcourt Brace Jovanovich, 1955), p. 54.

4. J. Alan Kay (Ed.), *Wesley's Prayers and Praises* (London: The Epworth Press, 1958), p. 65.

Chapter Nine

1. I have read many books on war, violence, and human nature. The most helpful have been J. Glenn Gray, *The Warriors: Reflections on Men in Battle* and Erich Fromm, *The Anatomy of Human Destructiveness.* Gray's book is unfortunately out of print. If you can find a copy, it will provide you with penetrating insights from the viewpoint of a professional soldier turned philosopher.

2. Carlo Carretto, *The God Who Comes* (New York: Orbis Books, 1974), p. 140.

3. Paul Tournier, *The Violence Within* (New York: Harper and Row, 1977), p. 59.

4. *Ibid.*, p. 76.

5. Dag Hammarskjöld, *Markings* (New York: Alfred A. Knopf, 1981), p. 142.

Chapter Ten

1. Jean-Pierre de Caussade, *Abandonment to Divine Providence* (New York: Image Books, 1975), John Beevers (tr.), p. 66.

2. *Ibid.*, p. 26.

3. Benedict J. Groeschel, *Spiritual Passages* (New York: Crossroad, 1984), p. 22.

4. Murray Bodo, *The Way of St. Francis* (New York: Image Books, 1985), p. 85.

5. Richard Wurmbrand, *Sermons in Solitary Confinement* (London: Hodder and Stoughton, 1969), pp. 58-59.

Chapter Eleven

1. Thomas à Kempis, *Meditations on the Life of Christ* (Grand Rapids: Baker Book House, 1978), p. 45.

2. Donald P. McNeill (et. al.), *Compassion* (New York: Doubleday and Company, Inc., 1982), pp. 66-67.

Chapter Twelve

1. Thomas Merton, *Bread in the Wilderness* (Collegeville: The Liturgical Press, 1953), p. 113.

2. Gerald G. May, *Will and Spirit: A Contemplative Psychology* (San Francisco: Harper and Row, Publishers, 1982), chapter 1.

3. *Ibid.*, p. 6.

4. Anthony de Mello, *The Song of the Bird* (New York: Image

Books, 1984), p. 60.

5. C.S. Lewis, *Mere Christianity* (New York: The Macmillan Company, 1960), p. 153.